A Place at the Table

Scripture, Sexuality, and Life in the Church

Kenneth D. Thurow

iUniverse, Inc.

New York   Bloomington

A Place at the Table
Scripture, Sexuality, and Life in the Church

The views expressed in this work are solely those of the author and do not necessarily reflect the views of the publisher, and the publisher hereby disclaims any responsibility for them.
iUniverse books may be ordered through booksellers or by contacting:

iUniverse
1663 Liberty Drive
Bloomington, IN 47403
www.iuniverse.com
1-800-Authors (1-800-288-4677)

Because of the dynamic nature of the Internet, any Web addresses or links contained in this book may have changed since publication and may no longer be valid. The views expressed in this work are solely those of the author and do not necessarily reflect the views of the publisher, and the publisher hereby disclaims any responsibility for them.

ISBN: 978-1-4401-1330-7 (pbk)
ISBN: 978-1-4401-1331-4 (ebk)

Library of Congress Control Number: 2009920622

Printed in the United States of America

iUniverse rev. date: 1/13/09

Dedicated to the memory of

Pastor Norval Hegland

friend and mentor

whose passion for justice ignited fires

that continue to burn

A PLACE AT THE TABLE

People yearn to have a place at the table – the place of diplomacy, the place of negotiation, the place of dialogue, the place of empowerment. At the table you have a voice, the right to participate and to shape decisions. At the table you are not devalued or disdained. As new nations came into being at the end of the colonial period, leaders who had been excluded were able to come to the table.

People yearn to have a place at the table – the family place of inclusion, the place of belonging, the place of warmth and intimacy, the place where bread is broken and hearts are joined. The table is the ultimate place of family togetherness, where nourishment and nurture are present in equal measure. The prodigal is welcomed with music and dancing and a feast, the alienated finds a powerful symbol of reconciliation, the one who was excluded or rejected is home and the circle is again complete.

People yearn to have a place at the table – The Table – where bread and wine are shared, where Christ is present to nourish with his presence, his body broken for us, his blood poured out for us. The table is the place where we are drawn into a Holy Communion with the Lord and with one another. The table is the place where we are invited to *see* one another, greet one another, embrace one another as sisters and brothers who know how profoundly we are embraced by abundant grace.

This book is about the table, about a place for many who have known rejection or only qualified welcome. It is about a place at the table in all three senses described above. It is, in a sense, a plea that sexual orientation or gender identity not be a hindrance to full recognition and acceptance in society or in the church. It is a plea that empty chairs at family tables be filled by the family members who once were estranged or excluded. It is a plea that the church which proclaims welcome and reconciliation would welcome these sisters and brothers to the table, whether with hands open to receive or vested, presiding, and serving the Sacrament.

> *For by grace you have been saved through faith, and this is not your own doing; it is the gift of God – not the result of works, so that no one may boast.*
>
> Ephesians 2:8-9

Table of Contents

Introduction

This book is neither memoir nor handbook. It is not "the story of my success" in ministry, nor the story of events by which I was transformed or reborn, nor a "how-to" manual. It is not the story of individuals you will meet along the way, although their part in it is significant. It is, if you will pardon the expression, "pastoral theology." As such, it deals with three inter-related topics, two – or maybe all three – of which arouse strong passions and generate controversy: the Bible, sexuality (especially non-heterosexuality), and how those two are related to the church's great mission and purpose in the world.

It is a book about how the Bible is understood, preached, and taught in congregations. Bible Studies in many congregational and "independent" settings have the goal of confirming participants in the faith. An unintended consequence is that the Bible comes to be regarded as an answer book, reinforcing what the participants have already been taught to think and believe; which is sometimes a good thing and sometimes not. In other settings, the Bible (if it is read at all) may be viewed as a book of myths and legends promoting violence and prejudice, with the result that the baby goes out with the bathwater. Probably worst of all, many with long backgrounds in the church will recall the plethora of "fill in the blanks" Bible Study materials of an earlier generation, leaving the overwhelming impression that the Bible is dull.

But the Bible is not dull; and though it contains many disquieting passages, I remain convinced that it is not a promoter of violence or prejudice. And it is not an "answer book" to confirm us in old attitudes and guide us in following old ruts. The chapters of this book dealing with my approach to Scripture are based on a lifetime of taking this book seriously, including 45 years of parish ministry. If there has been one consistent response to my preaching and teaching, it is that I somehow make the Bible come alive. To me, that means only that I don't get in the way, but that I know the biblical story and let the energy and the humor and the lively conversation *within* the Bible be seen. I hope that approach will also be apparent to readers of this book.

So, it is a book about the Bible. It is also a book about sexuality and the varieties of sexual orientation and gender identity existing within the membership of congregations. Sexuality is a powerful reality in our lives, and a pervasive influence in our society. Homosexuality has been one of the dominant topics of conversation in the Evangelical Lutheran Church in America (hereafter: ELCA) and other denominations for decades, a cause of frustration, separation, and disagreements both covert and overt.

This book is aimed most specifically at my own denomination. It contains anecdotes and historical fragments taken from my own experience in the ELCA, and specific recommendations for action in that denomination at all levels from congregation to what we, in our denomination, refer to as "Churchwide." But there is so much commonality in the way the struggle is taking place in virtually all denominations that readers of nearly any background, as well as readers who simply have an interest in the issue and in the cultural battles taking place in American society, will find it relevant to their context.

In this book I am speaking primarily to people who care about other people, who care about the issues prominent in society today, and who care about the Bible and the church. Caring about other people is the most basic. If you don't care, the book is not for you. It is late in 2008 as this book is heading for publication; California has just passed Proposition 8, and other states have similarly acted to restrict the rights and the lives of LGBTQ citizens. My reactions were – in order – surprise, then anger, then sadness. The passage of such measures is undoubtedly mean-spirited, but I am well aware that such a term does not characterize all the people who voted for the measures. There are many who voted, almost on auto-pilot, on the basis of long-established and traditional prejudice, and many others who believed that they were acting in faithfulness to church, to Bible, to God. This book is most specifically addressed to that audience, in the hope that through individual reading and reflection, and through group study and discussion, hearts and minds can be opened and the power of the gospel can have full effect.

The portions of this book focused on sexuality have a clear and firm perspective, but above all the presentation is intended to remind you of what you already know and lead you to think about people you already know – to draw attention to the things that are known to us in our family circles and our civic communities, as well as from the social sciences.

At some points in the text, the designation "LGBTQ" (Lesbian, Gay, Bisexual, Transgendered, Queer) appears, at other points I simply trust you to remember this wider application as you read. I might point out that the term, "queer," once used by heterosexuals as an insulting term, is now the self-designation preferred by some individuals who are not heterosexual. Lesbian, gay, bisexual, transgendered, and queer are neither strangers nor members of some frightening and perverse race. Research reveals that sexual orientation exists on a continuum; that is, that degrees of same-sex and other-sex attraction are to be found in each of us. In other words, sexual orientation is not a strictly black-and-white, either-or phenomenon. And, although the text makes clear that varieties of non-heterosexual orientation are included, most of the public discussion and controversy is framed as an issue of "homosexuality," a term which, therefore, appears frequently.

A brief disclaimer: although the book contains references to transgender, that subject is not dealt with clearly, fairly, or extensively. My experience in that area is limited and a good deal of it second-hand. The issue deserves a more complete treatment from someone more competent to address it. I would simply emphasize that these are also people who should find acceptance, understanding, and welcome in the church.

It has been observed that part of the zeitgeist of our time and culture is that people give little credence to information or logic. In political issues and culture wars, reality is irrelevant. The slogan of the '60s, "Don't trust anyone over thirty," has borne some distasteful fruit, becoming in this era, "Don't trust anyone." Trust only your own mind, your own emotions, your own gut. Make your own decisions and take your own stands. As a result, this is an age for testimony rather than dogma. With that awareness, I offer this book. It tells you how I read the Bible, as a lively book containing lively conversation and inviting us to participate. The book in your hands tells you how I regard the issues of sexual orientation and gender identity. And it presents what I see as a central feature of Jesus' ministry and a unique characteristic of the Christian mission presented in the New Testament: radical inclusivity. It is my testimony.

This would seem an appropriate point at which to outline my background and credentials. I am a pastor in the ELCA, a graduate of Wartburg Theological Seminary, with long experience in parish ministry. While active in parish ministry, I also served during the 1980s as an occasional biblical lecturer and workshop leader in South Dakota and Minnesota on behalf of the SHALOM Center for Continuing Theological Education.

I have been deeply involved in denominational matters, serving on the National Church Council of the American Lutheran Church from 1971-1980. During that term of service, I was selected to serve on the denomination's Ad Hoc Committee on Clergy Roster and Call Procedures, and served two terms on the Council's Program Review Committee. I served on the Executive Committee of the South Dakota District (ALC) and Synod (ELCA), and on the Synod Council of the Rocky Mountain Synod (ELCA).

High school classmate and sweetheart Marlys Thompson and I married in 1956. We have three children and six grandchildren. Marlys earned her B.A. in Education in 1972 and her M.A. in 1980. She taught in South Dakota, Illinois, and Colorado, primarily in the field of Special Education.

When I first entered parish ministry, it was my extreme good fortune to have, as my two geographically nearest clergy colleagues, Pastor Norval Hegland (to whom this book is dedicated) and Pastor Luther Johnson (who later took part in voter registration in the Mississippi Delta, and served inner-city ministries in Kansas City and Denver), both excellent theologians and passionate advocates for justice. I remain in their debt.

In the early years of my ministry, a church member I will call Sarah asked for an appointment. Sarah was a familiar face. She was frequently present at worship, but was not a participant in other programs or activities of the congregation. The purpose of her visit was to tell me that she had a partner. I do not recall that she even used the word, "lesbian," but she did make it clear that theirs was a loving, committed relationship. She wanted nothing more – simply to be known and accepted. In my memory I believe I did convey understanding and acceptance, or maybe only tolerance. But even if my memory is accurate, my response was minimal. Today I look back at Sarah's visit with admiration for her courage, and appreciation for the small but significant role she played in my education.

That encounter, and many others, helped to force a process of integrating new thoughts and insights with things that had always mattered deeply to me: serious study of Scripture and of traditional and deeply-ingrained Lutheran theology. Portions of this book were first written as essays and were shared with small numbers of acquaintances. Their positive response and urging have led me to offer this book in the hope that it might prompt reflection, offer new lines of thought, and engender conversation.

Clearly, how the Bible is to be read and interpreted is at the core of the church's consideration of the issue of homosexuality, or, more accurately, the spectrum of non-heterosexuality. The biblical witness on the matter is not extensive, but seems to many to be persuasive, even absolute. Christian tradition has, until recently, been quite uniform in viewing non-heterosexuality as disgusting, inappropriate, *evil.* Even today, a growing number of church structures and congregations, but very few denominations, have taken a more accepting stance in regard to persons previously excluded.

The title of the book reflects the climate of the late 20th and early 21st centuries, in which there is and has been an ongoing struggle for the non-heterosexual minority to gain a place at the table. In Congress, and in scattered state legislatures and municipal boards and councils, the presence of non-heterosexuals is a slowly growing phenomenon. In corporations such as Coors, Celestial Seasonings, and a host of others, same-gender partnerships are being recognized and employee benefits offered to such partners. But efforts persist to write the denial of such acceptance into law. "Gay-bashing", presented under such euphemisms as "defense of marriage" is a popular sport of legislators in state after state. Definitions of marriage as "between one man and one woman" take time and energy from more important issues, to say nothing of taking space on ballots. Within this book is a plea that minority sexual orientation and gender identity not stand as barriers to all the rights and privileges of citizenship and family life.

Further, it is a sad reality that issues of sexual orientation and gender identity continue to fracture families. Young persons continue to be excluded from their families, and some to suffer beatings, for being lesbian or gay. In family after family, long-standing alienation continues between siblings as family members cling to or struggle with their prejudices. It is my hope and prayer that people who read this book will be prompted to open the conversation, pick up the phone, pass the word through family networks, send a card – in short, do anything that will offer a first move toward reconciliation and toward a family table where every chair is filled.

And, though we may sing, "Mine is the church where everybody's welcome"[1] or "All are welcome in this place,"[2] it is my perception that the church, rather than leading the move toward reconciliation and acceptance, is actually lagging behind society, hesitant to fully embrace its own theology and to welcome those who have been long excluded, or whose participation has been restricted.

Attendance was small because of a blizzard. The Bishop was there, but instead of the 50-75 expected, scarcely a dozen of us were there to hear and talk about faith and life and ministry. In that small group, a young woman was brave enough to tell of her pain. She had been a life-long member of her congregation, baptized, confirmed, involved. She was one of the lay leaders of the youth program, ... until she became fully aware of her sexual orientation, and talked to the pastor responsible for youth ministry, who spoke to the Senior Pastor, which led to her removal from any ministry involving the youth of the congregation. She continued to love the Lord, to love the church, to feel called to ministry in that place, and she had not acted – would not act – in any inappropriate way. But fear, prejudice, and maybe the fear of prejudice, had closed the door to a ministry for which her faith and her gifts had fully qualified her. The Bishop

1   Hesla, Bret. A Dazzling Bouquet, words and music by Bret Hesla, recorded by Bread for the Journey on a CD "Global Songs, Local Voices."
2   Haugen, Marty. All Are Welcome, words and music by Marty Haugen. Chicago: GIA Publications,1994.

– bless his courage – commended her faith and empathized with her pain, and expressed his hope that such attitudes would change. More than 20 years have elapsed, and in too many churches, the attitudes, or the fears, remain.

In this writing I critique those abiding attitudes and examine points of Scripture, theology, and science that have been presented as militating against greater acceptance of those who are other than heterosexual. It is my conviction that positions many churches have taken, and to which many churches still hold, are inconsistent and place the churches, and the people whose lives they impact, in untenable and unjust situations. In this book, I urge that non-heterosexual members who desire to live in love and faithfulness, and who desire to serve the church with their Spirit-distributed gifts, be welcomed at the table – *either side* of the table, that the body may be more whole.

This book, written in an accessible style and with an abundance of biblical citations, expresses my convictions regarding the relationship between sexuality and Scripture. Clearly, the issues are related in public discourse, with people lining up on the side of inclusion or exclusion based not only on their life experience or their reading of the social sciences, but often on their reading of the Bible. I attempt to point out that there can be a positive and constructive relationship between our discussion of the Bible and our discussion of sexuality. Careful and thoughtful consideration of sexuality – not only homosexuality, but the spectrum in which both heterosexuality and non-heterosexuality are embraced – can help us think through our approach to and understanding of the Bible. And a more careful and thoughtful consideration of the Bible can widen and enrich our perceptions and attitudes in the area of sexuality. Thus, this book about the Bible. This book about sex. This book about theology and mission.

In dealing with Scripture, simple questions have prodded my thinking – questions such as these: "Why is this said here?", "To what end is the line of argument presented in this passage leading?", "How does this text relate to that one?", "How does this relate to life in the world?", "What is revelatory and transformative in this text?", "What do we learn here of the nature and passion of God, and of the purpose of the Incarnation?", and "What is the vision toward which this drives or leads us?" The Lutheran Confessions have made a contribution, especially the passages addressing the issue of mandatory celibacy of priests.

Along the way, I have been blessed by the insights and arguments of others, those with whom I disagree as well as those whose insights and understandings are compatible with the results of my own study and reflection. I have found life experience to be a great teacher. Greatly varied articles and lectures representing all positions on the issues have made their contribution. The program in human sexuality presented by the University of Minnesota in the 1970s was helpful in addressing many issues related to sexuality. I regret that I cannot recall and list the many lectures and editorial columns that have stimulated my thinking. The bibliography at the end of the book includes several of the many printed works which have contributed to my thought process, and which I gratefully acknowledge.

My special thanks to Dr. Frank Benz, Dr. Ann Fritschel, and clergy colleagues from the Boulder-Broomfield Conference of the ELCA's Rocky Mountain Synod: Pastors Laurel Alexander, Steve Berke, Joel Brandt, Martin Lettow, and Inga Oyan Longbrake for reading the manuscript and offering suggestions; to the members of Prince of Peace (North Logan, UT), whose warmth and openness in discussion paved the way for the writing of this book; and to members of Holy Trinity (Littleton, CO), Lutheran Church of Hope (Broomfield, CO), Zion Lutheran (Limon, CO), Resurrection (Lakewood, CO), Shepherd of the Hills (Boulder, CO), and others who have participated with me in study of these issues; to Pastor Leonard Rudolph for forwarding to me the e-mail quoted at the beginning of the chapter on "Abomination"; to Andrea Griffiths and Lauri Muller, who have taught me much and whose friendship I treasure; and above all to my wife, Marlys, for her encouragement, her shared commitment to the goal of inclusion, and her patience in helping to provide me with time and space for writing.

Unless otherwise noted, Scripture quotations are from the New Revised Standard Version (NRSV).

Chapter 1
Homosexuality and the Church

I missed seeing the Olympic Torch! It was the winter of 2002, and the Olympic Torch was coming through our town en route to the Salt Lake City Winter Olympics. But a phone call had come that afternoon. Could I find time to meet with two young women who had been visiting our congregation? I expected something related to church teachings or membership procedures, possibly even personal problems. I made the appointment, and missed the passage of the Olympic Torch. The introductory conversation was brief. One was a "cradle Lutheran" with long and extensive involvement in the church, the other came from a different religious tradition but had also been deeply involved in her tradition. After brief introductory conversation, they came to the point: "We are looking for a church we can attend as a couple." Their agenda, their need, was on the table. And their orientation.

I welcomed them, assured them that I believed ours to be such a church. As we talked, I learned that they regularly prayed together, studied Scripture together, discussed and grew in faith, and cared for others to a truly inspiring degree. Both were employed at a long-term care facility, and (I later learned) when residents were hospitalized, would make hospital visits on their own time and without any specific encouragement to do so. Over a period of several months, their presence in our congregation touched hearts and changed attitudes. Before long, and with the congregation's full knowledge that this was a lesbian couple, one of them was asked to lead our congregation's Sunday high school class, and soon became one of the leaders of the community's ecumenical youth group. After several serious discussions of the faith, the non-Lutheran sought baptism and membership in the congregation. In the process of getting to know and respect this couple, the congregation acted to declare itself "Reconciling in Christ" – the Lutheran term indicating an official declaration of acceptance that includes people who are other than heterosexual.

The action was not unanimous, but passed by a huge majority and, as often happens, opened the door for many members to feel safe talking about LGBTQ persons in their circle of family and friends. The two young women were not some theoretical "they," but were fellow-believers, sisters in the faith. "They" were now "us."

Sexual orientation, specifically homosexuality, has been constantly in the news, "Massachusetts Supreme Judicial Court removes barriers to marriage of same-sex couples."[3] Politicians and legislative bodies consider laws or constitutional amendments that would overturn the decision or define (or "protect") marriage. Homosexuality is not only in the news, it is in the church news. "New Hampshire Episcopalians elect gay bishop." "Six in ten Americans oppose the Episcopal Church's decision to allow bishops to authorize blessings of same-sex unions, according to a *Washington Post* poll." The public dialog has been all about "them."

In the current climate in my denomination, the ELCA, as in the United Methodist Church, the Episcopal Church in the USA, the Presbyterian, Reformed, Baptist (I will not attempt an inclusive listing, but you get the point) and other church bodies; in American culture, in political battles taking place in legislatures, in

---

3   The decision, rendered November 18, 2003, in the case of *Goodridge vs. Department of Public Health*, declared the state's ban on same-sex marriage to be unconstitutional

2

the Congress, and in the courts, sex – particularly homosexuality – is a hot button issue. There is debate over whether to protect the civil rights and civil liberties of people who are not heterosexual; whether to permit civil unions, or marriage, or grant some legal status; whether to pass and enforce "hate crimes" laws and, if so, whether to have such laws cover sexual orientation as well as race and religion. Across the landscape stretches a minefield that in some way touches nearly all of us. And even if it does not, it has caught our attention and probably our passion as we pause to understand ourselves in relationship to the issues.

The ELCA is currently involved in a process of study, discussion, and discernment first intended to lead to a 2005 decision (but not decided in 2005 nor in 2007) as to whether the denomination will approve the blessing of same-sex unions and the ordination of homosexuals living in, or desiring the right to live in, committed relationships. Other denominations have ventured into the minefield and been wounded, or are trying to find ways either to address or to avoid the issue. What must be noted is that this is not a "top-down" process. In almost every case, and in almost every denomination, the impetus has come from the grassroots. For the Episcopal Church in the USA, the election of Bishop V. Eugene Robinson took place in the diocese of New Hampshire. The ELCA study was prompted by actions initiated by congregations and by resolutions passed in regional ("Synod") assemblies.

It should be pointed out that though the issue has been framed as concerning "homosexuality," "gay marriage," or the like, we are actually dealing with the entire phenomenon of sexuality, sexual orientation, and gender identity. At many points, perhaps most, what is said of homosexuality applies also to individuals who are bisexual, and transgendered.

It appears that in consideration of the topic, there are at least two great divides discernible in the American population. One is the generational divide. Though both acceptance and condemnation of homosexual behavior can be found in all age groups, there is a marked statistical difference between the attitudes of older and younger Americans, both in society at large and among Christians, with younger adults more accepting. The other divide is between Christians, especially more conservative and self-styled "evangelical" Christians, and the society at large. Again, the difference is statistical, with acceptance and rejection to be found in both groups, but with conservative Christians more likely to reject homosexual behaviors and homosexual unions.

But the question is complicated. Obviously, the issue of homosexuality is part of the larger issue of, well, *sexuality*, which is a very personal issue. Our responses to "sexuality" and to "homosexuality" involve both reason and emotion, and sometimes we are uncertain as to which is which. We have the challenge of understanding our own sexuality, and our awareness of its power. As adults, we have our own memories, guilts, and questions. We have been titillated and shamed by our sexuality. Quite possibly we are troubled by the blatant sexuality of our culture in which "sex sells."

We have been challenged and troubled by the changing mores of our society. Our parents or our siblings or our children have been divorced. Possibly our own marriages have not endured. A sizeable percentage of our children have been sexually active. A huge majority of couples live together before – or completely apart from – marriage. A couple of decades back, the term POSSLQ crept into US Census statistics: "Persons of Opposite Sex Sharing Living Quarters." I recently heard another one for the first time, "SE" – "Spousal Equivalent." And now *mother,* already drawing Social Security, has moved in with her boyfriend? And you say we're not in Kansas anymore? Oh, yes, we are, but Kansas has also become unrecognizable.

But many adults have grudgingly acquiesced to the idea of the kids who "live together." They are coming to be viewed as normal, and their parents retain hopes and dreams of grandchildren. That dream seems to be built into our genetic code. Long ago a geneticist (partly tongue in cheek … I think?) commented that a chicken is one egg's way of making another egg. It is often on the ground of this view of its "normality" that cohabitation of young adults is accepted. And mother is "normal" (after all, she had me). But perhaps, with sexuality bustin' out all over the place, perhaps it is time – past time – to pull in the reins, draw a line in the sand, put *some kind of limits* on the whole thing.

And into this mix come "PFLAG" and "LGBTQ" and "Gay Pride" parades and "Queer Eye for the Straight Guy." At the moment I do not recall who said, "I don't care what you do, just so you don't do it in the street and scare the horses," perhaps you remember. But there are many in my circle of acquaintance who believe that non-heterosexuals are now scaring the horses. "Isn't it time, and isn't this the place, at which society should choose to limit sexuality?" some would ask.

Another complicating factor in our discussions of homosexuality is that causation is unknown; which is true for all varieties of sexuality. *Hetero*sexuality, after all, just *is*. We assume it is genetic, but have no proof. Many assume *homo*sexuality is genetic, but have no proof. A further complication is that there are no hard-and-fast fences or dividing lines separating orientations. There are no visible, physical markers identifying one's sexual orientation. Some believe homosexuality results from experiences in early childhood, or from bad parenting, or from having been misled during adolescence, or from individuals making wicked and perverse decisions by which they choose to be homosexual. The difficulty is that we do not know with any degree of scientific certainty.

Moreover, if it is seen as a problem, we don't know how to fix it or whether it needs to be fixed. Some attempts at counseling or reprogramming report varying degrees of "success", but the percentages are not large and occur almost exclusively in work with persons who enter the programs with a strong desire to change their orientation, or, at least, their ability to express themselves sexually. Other research indicates that very few homosexuals have a desire to change or can make lasting changes. And we are left with this: homosexuality *is*.

But some related statistics are disturbing. Homosexuals are often rejected by family members; in adolescence, they commit suicide at an alarming rate; in schools they are sometimes subjected to mocking or physical assaults; and, statistics say, more non-heterosexuals tend toward promiscuous life-styles than is true of heterosexuals. And, in Wyoming, Matthew Shepard was beaten and left to die because he was gay. One word of caution should be expressed in regard to the issue of promiscuity: our society is constantly exposed to the message that promiscuity among heterosexuals is to be accepted if not expected.

And yet, most of us have LGBTQ persons as family members, friends, or members of our congregations. Many of us know gay or lesbian couples who have lived quietly, "normally", and apparently faithfully for years. Some of us know homosexual couples who are rearing children or have reared children, not uncommonly heterosexual children. On the other hand, we know heterosexuals with the same profiles – some promiscuous, some faithful, some having been married multiple times, some quiet, "normal", apparently faithful for years.

But in regard to the stance of the church *vis a vis* homosexuality, the issue as we face it is not single-faceted. Many who raised the issues, many who live in faith and with alternative sexual identities, many who have friends or family members who are LGBTQ, are less concerned with "what the Bible says" than with their own life experience or the experience of individuals they know and love. And some, such as many New Hampshire Episcopalians, have looked at the issue and have boldly (or baldly) gone where no major denomination has knowingly gone before. It is most certainly true that there have been gay – and, more recently, lesbian – clergy in virtually every denomination, and quite probably gay bishops as well. But such individuals have been "closeted". What is new is the fact that the Episcopal Church in the USA has acted openly and in full knowledge of the situation, and that other denominations are giving consideration to taking similar stances.

As we consider the whole topic we must examine ourselves and inquire into our "heart of hearts". And we (speaking to the heterosexual majority) are left with no recourse but to make decisions, decisions based more on who *we* are than on who the members of the minority community are. To what degree and in what areas are we prepared to accept, even welcome, those who are LGBTQ in our lives, our neighborhoods, our churches? Would we grant them the right to live with safety and with human rights assured: jobs, housing, etc., etc.? Would we grant them the opportunity for intimacy? For secure, long-term, committed relationships? Or do our attitudes actually reflect a desire that if they do not disappear they should be eliminated? That last question may sound harsh, but many statements made in public media and in church circles concerning homosexuals would seem to point toward that conclusion.

The whole issue of homosexuality, (or, more accurately, non-heterosexuality), and not only the actions taken and studies undertaken, is troubling to many, and strikes a good many Christians as not only troubling, not only inappropriate for the church to consider, but as completely, at its root, sinfully *wrong*! Some Christians are troubled on the basis of old-fashioned fear and prejudice; others on the basis of the visceral reaction that it "just feels wrong". Some are moved by actual life experiences and others on acquired understandings based on events such as the ongoing furor over revelations of pedophilia or homosexuality among Roman Catholic priests. But a great many Christians hold their objections on the basis of specific biblical passages and traditional Christian teaching.

In the midst of a discussion of sexuality at the 2002 Rocky Mountain Synod (ELCA) Assembly, a friend commented to me that the current debate over sexuality, including whether to approve ceremonies of commitment between same-sex partners and whether to make possible the ordination of homosexuals who are in committed relationship, cannot be settled on the basis of the Bible. The fact that in the "committed relationship" debate both proponents and opponents appeal to Scripture would indicate that my friend is right. But that does not mean Scripture is irrelevant. In the current discussion I have heard some church members advocate "moving beyond Scripture" and others defend what they see as the plain meaning of biblical texts. I would prefer to invite both camps, and people in neither camp, to do more serious study and reflection to see what is in and behind the texts.

For people of faith, dealing with the issues of other than heterosexual orientation has involved a good deal of wrestling with conflicting values. More than that, the discussion of these issues has exposed the wide variety of ways the Bible is read and interpreted in congregations, in denominations, and by individuals.

Most faith communities see themselves as places of love, compassion, and ministry; places where there is welcome for all, and especially for the "troubled and penitent." Knowing that one measure of Christian obedience is ministry to "the least of these," (Matthew 25) congregations care for many who have been overlooked or rejected by society. The homeless, the poor, single parents, the imprisoned, the addicted, the divorced, the abused, the HIV/AIDS patient – the list is long, and in reality much longer than delineated here. The church is a place of ministry, and in ways beyond number the wounded and broken-hearted are met with compassionate ministry.

But the church has also traditionally played a large role in addressing moral and ethical issues in the arena that is often referred to as prophetic. It is in this aspect of the church's proclamation that a great divide appears. I will attempt a simple statement, realizing that it will be, to some degree, a caricature. At one pole are churches that focus on sharpening lines, calling for changes in behavior, exhorting individuals to "cross over" and leave destructive or doubtful behaviors behind. The list of such behaviors differs by denomination, congregation, pastor, and individual. In the current climate, non-heterosexual orientation and behavior are on many lists. At the other pole are churches that focus on erasing the lines, calling for greater acceptance of diversity and greater understanding of the pervasiveness of sin and the reconciling power of grace. In this thumbnail sketch one can perceive the tension over sexual orientation. Should the church, and individuals, attempt to suppress and convert, or accept and embrace? The answer, of course, will rest not only on the simple question of orientation, but on one's assumptions as to what is implied by orientation. Does non-heterosexual orientation equate to promiscuity, pedophilia, an attempt to harm or recruit the vulnerable, including children? Those questions will be addressed later in this book.

What is a Christian to do, think, or say? People who hold to the first of the views sketched out above often describe their stance as "love the sinner, hate the sin." But that statement begs the question: just what is defined as the sin, and why is it so defined? And people who are painfully aware that they are the ones referred to as sinners in that traditional phrase often find little they can identify as love in the attitudes they encounter. In response, they may point to the words of St. Paul in Romans, "in passing judgment on another, you condemn yourself." As you are no doubt aware by now, the listing of verses to which one can appeal in defending either of the opposing positions can be expanded without bringing a clear resolution. In *Fiddler on the Roof*,[4] the lead character, named Tevye, tries to come to terms with his youngest daughter's love for a Russian, one not only outside the community, but outside the faith. He ponders "on the one hand..., on the other hand..., on the other hand..." until he realizes that his faith and conviction leave no alternative and he declares, "there is no other hand!" Similarly, many in the

---

4   Stein, Joseph, music by Jerry Bock, lyrics by Sheldon Harnick. <u>Fiddler on the Roof</u>. New York: Crown Publishing, 1964. Dialog from Act II

church are considering alternatives, while others declare, "there is no other hand."

All of which has invited many to study, think, comment, and write. In the spirit of St. Luke, "it has seemed good to me also" to set out the results of my thoughts, prayers, and study.

Let me begin here. Sexuality is part of our human identity; a powerful, unavoidable, delightful, perhaps sometimes frightening, quality of our personhood having bodily form and inextricably linked to our minds, emotions, and experiences. We are sexual beings. But we are not identical sexual beings. Not only are we two kinds of sexual beings, male and female, but we are as individual, as unique, as our faces, our bodies, our feelings – perhaps as varied as our fingerprints.

Sexuality exists on a continuum. Anyone with access to Ann Landers, Dear Abby, Dr. Ruth, or TV is familiar with the oft-heard plaint of the woman or man whose spouse has lost interest in sex, and with the occasional plaint of one whose spouse is "over-sexed". Sexuality is part of the life of children, sometimes to the discomfort of their parents; and of senior citizens in the latest chapters of life, sometimes to the discomfort of their adult children. And we learn from such sources and from our own experience that the great majority of people are sexually attracted to members of the opposite sex: females attracted to males, males to females. But that, too, is on a continuum, or should we say a bell-shaped curve very heavily weighted toward opposite-sex attraction. Some, however, find themselves attracted, or potentially attracted, to members of both sexes; some are attracted more specifically to members of their own sex.

The number is unknown. The oft-heard claim that 10% of the population is "homosexual" has apparently been based on Kinsey's studies,[5] which found that, at the time of the studies, about 10% of the population reported having had "homosexual" experiences. Studies of sexuality, even more than most research

---

5   Kinsey, A. C., W. B. Pomeroy, and C. E. Martin. <u>Sexual Behavior in the Human Male</u>. Philadelphia: Saunders, 1948.

studies, seem to be skewed by the questions, approaches, and biases of the researchers. So, we do not know. In any case, the statistic is irrelevant. Nothing I say in this book depends on the numbers.

As a matter of simple information the question, "what is homosexuality?" is easy to answer: homosexuality is sexual attraction to a person or persons of one's own gender. But such an answer, while accurate, explains nothing. Perhaps we must expand the question by asking, "How shall we characterize or understand homosexuality"? To this question several possible responses are put forward, reflecting differing perspectives. For my purposes, I will work with four. I will begin with the most negative view and work toward the more positive.

The first possible response is that homosexuality is a wicked perversity, a chosen immorality that offends against God and seeks to make others into victims or to subvert (pervert?) them into making similar wicked and sinful choices and carrying on similar evil behaviors. This is the stance taken by some 80 nations of the world in which homosexuality is still criminalized. If "wicked perversity" is the basic reality of homosexuality, the appropriate response of individuals and society is clear. Homosexuality should be suppressed in every way possible; homosexuals restricted in their contact with others and particularly kept from contact with those who may be weaker or more impressionable, including children and adolescents; and homosexuals who act in accord with their sexual preference deserve society's punishments. The role of society is to suppress and perhaps imprison homosexuals. The role of the church is to seek conversion, a change of heart and behavior, in the spirit of "turn from your wickedness and live".

A second possible response is that to be other than heterosexual is a devastating misfortune, a scarring in mind and emotion resulting from events and influences to which one has been subjected. Perhaps the influence was bad parenting, or childhood sexual abuse, or unfortunate bonding with the wrong parent as a result of the other parent being distant, abusive, alcoholic, or absent. In this understanding, homosexuals are victims, scarred in the way a burn victim or a survivor of rape or traumatic stress might be. Though such victims are to be viewed with compassion, it is appropriate that efforts be undertaken to prevent unhealthy or inappropriate choices and responses. In this view there may be the perception that homosexuals in non-celibate relationships are acting in destructive ways that should be restrained through teaching, persuasion, counseling, and prayer. The role of society is then to provide resources for "treatment" or counseling; with more severe treatment assigned to those who do not respond. The role of the church might then be seen as offering empathetic support and therapy, so that the individual might be healed and be able to live a healthy, normal, productive life.

The third of the four possible responses to homosexuality considered here is that homosexuality might be seen as one result of the Fall of humans into sin – a genetic or psychic flaw comparable to diabetes, myopia, some forms of mental illness, or any of a host of other conditions or pre-dispositions. This view takes seriously the concept that the world in which we live is no longer Eden, and that the whole creation yearns "to be set free from its bondage to decay". This view would hold that, though not in accord with God's intention in creation, such conditions are real, do exist, but do not by themselves constitute immorality or indicate guilt before God.

In this view, those who are not heterosexual, like individuals with any number of other conditions, would be understood to live with a reality that falls under the rubric of human burden rather than human rebellion. LGBTQ persons could then be seen as living with their own set of realities; their own gifts and problems; their own Creator-given needs for community, relationship and intimacy; and with the challenge to live godly lives in love and faithfulness just as do all others within the body of Christ. In this scenario, the role of the heterosexual majority in society is to accept those with other sexual orientations as individuals with their own uniqueness and their own burdens, and guarantee all rights granted to all who are less than perfect. The role of the church is then to live with non-heterosexuals, as with all others, in community; loving, helping and praying for one another; and accepting the spiritual gifts, faithful relationships, and talents for ministry of all members of the body.

A fourth possible response is to see varieties of sexual orientation as one more manifestation of a creation bursting with variety. Within the animal kingdom are moles and moose and monkeys, hummingbirds and hawks and herons, octopi and ospreys and ocelots; within the plant kingdom are rye and redwoods and roses. At every turn we see incredible variety. To which we might add that some researchers report apparent "homosexuality" in animal species in approximately the same proportion as among humans. The role of society and church is then to accept homosexuality as one more facet of normality in a complicated and incredibly diverse world, and, in the church, to encourage the faith and the gifts of any whom the Spirit might call to membership and to ministry.

In a later chapter we will look at what the Bible has to say, and will review the most relevant passages in some detail. But it would be appropriate at this point to see what contribution the Lutheran Confessions might make to the conversation.

In the strictest sense, Luther and the Confessions add little to the discussion of homosexuality. The topic is not referenced in the Confessions, though some phrasings *may* have it in mind, as in Luther's statements on the sixth Commandment in his Large Catechism. There, in his critique of the mandatory celibacy of priests, he refers to supposed celibates who "either indulge in open and shameless fornication or secretly do even worse – things too evil to mention".[6] The very limited references in Luther's writings, as in his biblical commentaries, uphold the basic stance

---

6   Quotation from Luther's Large Catechism from pages 393-394 of Tappert, Theodore G. The Book of Concord. Philadelphia: Muhlenberg Press, 1959.

of traditional Christian biblical interpretation and teaching, regarding homosexuality as sinful and condemnable.

But the Confessions are relevant at another point: in their insistence that celibacy is unnatural except for the few who have the gift. In the same explanation of the Sixth Commandment in his Large Catechism, Luther praises marriage, then writes: "Yet there are some (although few) exceptions whom God has especially exempted – some who are unsuited for married life and others whom he has released by a high supernatural gift so that they can maintain chastity outside of marriage. Where nature has its way, as God implanted it, it is not possible to remain chaste outside of marriage; for flesh and blood remain flesh and blood, and the natural inclinations and stimulations have their way without let or hindrance, as everyone's observation and experience testify", and he speaks of those who "resist God's order and commandment when they despise and forbid marriage, and boast that they will maintain perpetual chastity...." Similar arguments are made throughout the Confessions.

We might note especially Luther's reference to "few exceptions" and "a high supernatural gift so that they can maintain chastity outside of marriage." This should in no way be understood as an argument that Martin Luther or the other authors of the Confessions wrote in defense of homosexuality. As stated above, there is little doubt that they held the same unchallenged, negative views of homosexuality as their predecessors and contemporaries. The point here is that their understanding of creation and human nature led them to oppose any ecclesiastical or legal demands that were contrary to flesh-and-blood realities. They affirmed that humans are sexual beings, and that attempts to suppress sexuality have unhealthy consequences.

Today "observation and experience testify" to the existence of a variety of sexual orientations and gender identities. For these persons, also, "flesh and blood remain flesh and blood." The wisdom of the Confessions should make us reluctant to maintain that (a) non-heterosexuals may not marry (nor establish equivalent, recognized unions) but (b) must nevertheless remain celibate or live under the judgment and rejection of "normal" and "moral" people. As one who can see merit in both the third and fourth of the views described above, I think it not only appropriate, but long overdue, that the church act in accord with its basic gospel principles in granting full acceptance to lesbian, gay, bisexual and transgendered Christians on the same terms as it accepts heterosexual Christians.

Newscasts reporting the decision of the Massachusetts Supreme Judicial Court interviewed homosexuals in enduring relationships – in one case, 32 years, in another, more than 16 years. The first homosexual couple married in San Francisco (all the same-sex marriages were subsequently annulled by California courts) was a lesbian couple who had been together 50 years. The first same-sex couple married in California in 2008 was an elderly lesbian couple. I have met a gay couple who have been together for 37 years. Individuals who are homosexual have been deeply spiritual and deeply committed members of most of the congregations I have served as pastor. In conversation, church members, church musicians, and others have testified to the personal qualities and the significant gifts possessed and contributed by their gay and lesbian friends, students, and (yes) pastors.

These are persons who work, pay taxes, worship, receive the Eucharist, care for others, and give of themselves to the welfare of the community. Some rear children. In short, they are just like you and me except, perhaps, for what takes place in their bedrooms. And, truth be told, I don't care to spend a great deal of thought on what any, including my *heterosexual* neighbors and acquaintances, do in their bedrooms.

Studies have proliferated – studies of the phenomenon of homosexuality and studies of biblical references to same-sex relationships. Scholars differ in their understandings of the context of biblical passages. Some question whether the passages can be understood to address long-term, loving, committed relationships. But if the biblical text is taken at face value, those biblical passages which deal with conduct we would recognize as homosexual seem clear in rejecting and condemning such behavior. Extensive analyses of the texts appear in a study done by Dr. Ed. Miller of the University of Colorado (*Homosexuality and the Bible*) and in a book by Dr. Robert A. J. Gagnon of Pittsburgh Theological Seminary (*The Bible and Homosexual Practice*).

Their analyses of the texts, the vocabulary, and the culture in which the texts were composed make the point clear to almost every reader: the biblical texts which reference same-gender sexual activity uniformly reject and condemn such sexual expression. The Genesis story of Lot's visitors (though variously interpreted elsewhere in Scripture), the laws of Leviticus, the letters of Paul, in short, all the specific texts which clearly involve same-sex sexual activity, share the same perspective: conduct we would term homosexual is strongly rejected, is regarded as an "abomination", to use a term from older translations. For a detailed analysis, I refer you to the studies cited.

Which, for many, concludes the argument and closes the subject. How, they ask, can the plain words of the Bible be explained or reinterpreted away? By the standards of the "reinterpreter", does anything in the Bible mean what it says? How can black be made white, condemnation turned to acceptance? The concerns are understandable, and may be based on attitudes learned in church and on long-held views of the Bible and of morality. But I would invite you to return to the previous paragraph and note the specific wording. I said, "specific texts which clearly involve same-sex sexual activity" and "conduct *we would term* homosexual". In taking a fresh biblical view, perhaps this strange statement can serve as a starting point: *In the Bible, there are no alcoholics, and no homosexuals.*

"But of course there are", you might say. "There are mentions of drunkards and of being drunk, and St. Paul urges his readers not to get drunk with wine. And Leviticus, Romans, and other texts condemn same-gender sexual activity." Right you are. The Bible knows that some drink too much alcohol, even do so frequently or regularly. And the Bible knows that some people continue in sexual practices that are seen as weird, or outside the norm. But the Bible never says, "alcoholic", and the Bible never says, "homosexual". There is no word that reflects an understanding of addiction or chemical imbalance corresponding to the modern term "alcoholism"; and no word reflecting the modern concept of sexual orientation. For both phenomena, there are only words describing behaviors. Both "alcoholic" and "homosexual" are words of recent origin,[7] and here is my point, *each of those words presents an alternative view of a phenomenon based on new understanding, awareness, and research.*

I do not mean to imply any similarity between "alcoholism" and "homosexuality." The phenomena cannot be compared to one another, but today we know that many whom the Bible calls "drunkards" are persons with an addiction to or intolerance for alcohol, and are in some important way unlike others who drink without being addicted and without such an intolerance. Most people today understand "alcoholism" and view "alcoholics" differently than the writers of the Bible viewed "drunkards". It is also true that the person who "lies with" another of the same gender has a sexual orientation which differs from the orientation of those who are sexually attracted to the opposite gender. Most people today view "homosexuality" differently than the writers of the Bible viewed the activities condemned in Leviticus, Romans, and other passages. It is not disregard for the Bible that has made the difference, it is new awareness of phenomena in our world and, therefore, new regard for our neighbor as she or he actually exists.

So, while the reading or quoting of texts closes the argument for some, for others it is one point at which to begin a process

---

7   "alcoholic" in 1890, "homosexual" in 1892, as words that could be applied to persons, according to Merriam-Webster's Collegiate Dictionary, 11th Edition, Springfield, MA 2005

of study, conversation, and discernment. For these, and I count myself among them, there are other questions to be addressed. For example, are we clear about the type and quality of same-gender relationships described in the Bible? To pose another question, are we being fair to the text if we pick from it those passages that declare same-sex conduct to be an "abomination" without analyzing other texts in which that word appears? That is to say, what if there are other "abominations" which we no longer regard in that light? Further, if we are bound to reject homosexuality on the basis of the biblical texts which deal with the subject, does that bind us to reject other things rejected in the Bible and to accept things accepted? Why or why not? Are the morals and ethics of Christians controlled by topical listings of texts? And, most importantly, on what rationale is our study of, and attitude toward, homosexuality limited to the texts in which the subject seems to be specifically addressed? Are there not other passages which are fully as relevant to the discussion?

Most Christians would agree that integrity in biblical study requires us to deal fairly with the plain meaning of texts. Most would also agree that integrity requires texts to be read in context: immediate textual context, historical and cultural context, wider context in which "Scripture interprets Scripture", and – not to be forgotten – the context in which the church interprets Scripture. In addition, when a text appears in the midst of a line of argument, integrity requires that we deal with the text with full regard for the totality of the argument, which *is* the context in such a situation.

Virtually every Christian tradition (whether consciously or not) has trusted the leading of the Holy Spirit to lead into all truth, to take the things of Christ and reveal them to us, in accord with the promise of Jesus in John 16. Virtually every tradition (to say nothing of every interpreter) makes its own decisions, when push comes to shove, as to which texts control which. A case in point might be the question of the role of women in the church. Do we give greater weight to, *"let women be silent"* (I Corinthians

14:34), or to *"there is no longer male and female"* (Galatians 3:28)? If we attempt to affirm both, how do we decide which passage actually controls our practice?

Do we approach Scripture with a desire to be consistent, with openness to the leading of the Spirit, with awareness that thought and study and scientific learning are also of God? Do we note passages in the Bible that challenge narrow or "status quo" thinking and burst open old wineskins with the power of new revelation? In what ways do we regard the words of the prophets, or of Jesus, or of St. Paul, as instructive for our approach to the Bible and to our world?

It appears to me that those who hold negative attitudes toward gays and lesbians hold those attitudes on a variety of bases. Some hold attitudes toward "varieties of sexual expression" on the basis of old-fashioned American fear and prejudice. Others hold their attitudes more or less tentatively as persons who know what they know and have seen what they have seen but who wish to leave the door ajar for new learnings or insights to enter. And some people are willing (and ready) to be more open but feel bound by what they have read or heard regarding the Bible and feel their consciences to be "captive to the word of God."

In the next chapter I invite you to join me in noting what the Bible says and why it says it. Because the objections based on Bible and conscience are commonly based on a list of specific "homosexuality" passages, we will look at those passages before proceeding to include other biblical material. Along the way, we will challenge you to review your own basis of understanding. Do you attempt to be, or desire to be, consistent in the way you read and use Scripture? Do you understand why one passage is more persuasive to you than another? Do you look for passages you agree with, or do you hope to change and grow as you study the Bible? Are some passages, some teachings, more central than others?

I encourage you to read with heart and mind open, and with the Spirit of Christ as your guide and companion.

Chapter 2
Reading the Words, Learning the Music

About 150 C.E., only decades after the last of the writings we know as the New Testament entered circulation in the early church, an astronomer named Ptolemy published what became his best-known work, illustrating the movement of sun and moon, stars and planets, around the earth – earth being understood to be the center of the universe. In 1543, thirteen years after the presentation of the Augsburg Confession and not long before the death of Martin Luther, Nicolaus Copernicus, a Polish-born astronomer, advanced the novel thesis that Earth was not the center of the universe, but that, in fact, the earth rotated on its axis and revolved around the sun. Still later, Galileo, astronomer and builder of telescopes, supported Copernicus and probed much further into the wonders of the solar system and the universe. For contradicting the teaching of the church, which was basically identical with the long-accepted view of Ptolemy and was supported by appeals to Scripture and reason, Galileo was condemned by the church.

The church's position is easy to understand. Numerous passages in the Bible declare the centrality and immovability of the earth. Moreover, our *experience* of the universe supports the position of the church. We *experience* our place in the universe as a stable platform – sometimes beset by natural disasters, to be sure – from which we observe an assortment of heavenly bodies moving across the dome of the sky. Acceptance of Copernicus and Galileo required a monumental shift in understanding not only of cosmology, but of Scripture and theology as well.

One of my oldest Bibles, one still on my shelf, includes under the chapter heading of Genesis 1 a date: 4006 B.C., the date of Creation. The date is not difficult to ascertain. Our calendar is based on a reckoning forward and backward from the birth of Jesus, a somewhat flawed reckoning, to be sure. We now know that the calculations were off by some 4-6 years. Prior dates have traditionally been labeled "B.C." (Before Christ), and later dates "A.D." (Anno Domini, "Year of our Lord"). Modern scholarship prefers the slightly more neutral designations "B.C.E.", for "Before the Common Era" and "C.E.", for "Common Era". Also, within a narrow margin of error, the reign of King David began about 1000 B.C., a date which can be learned from Jewish and other extra-biblical sources. For dates prior to David, one simply does the math. Nearly all the dates and ages of relevant personages can be found in the Bible. And the math results in a date of 4006 B.C. But this raises a question: do you believe creation occurred in 4006 B.C.? To be sure, there are some among us who hold to the literal truth of Genesis. Most of us, however, accept the verdict of science that the earth is much, much older, even though the Bible says otherwise.

So, why am I telling you this? Why these two historical snippets at the beginning of this chapter? Because the above illustrations are only two of many that could be used to remind us of shifts that have taken place in the church's reading of the Bible. In each case, what was written in the text came to be recognized as not the last word, not literally true, but rather a construct that reflected the age and culture in which the text was written. At those points the text has come to be seen as having theological and literary value rather than scientific or historical.

Yet that outcome has not reduced the value of the text for people willing to listen, reflect, and come to new understandings.

Might it be time for reflection and new understandings in regard to questions of sexual orientation and gender identity? Martin Luther, you may recall, insisted that "Popes and Councils can err." Is that also true of the church in the 21st century? What if there are people of faith in our congregations who are living "quiet and peaceable lives, in all godliness and dignity (I Timothy 2:2)," living with partners in love and faithfulness with deep yearnings to make those relationships legal and public? What if there are people who, in matters of sex, are loving and respectful of their partners, and who are in no way abusive or promiscuous? What if there are people who "sing, pray, and praise," who serve their neighbors, love the Lord, trust the grace of God, believe in "the forgiveness of sins, the resurrection of the body, and the life everlasting," and who are – what, red-haired, left-handed, near-sighted? No, of course not, but what if there are such people who are not heterosexual? In other words, what if the church has been wrong? What if we have accepted as divine judgment what was in reality the cultural convention of an earlier age? And what if the way we read the Bible has been part of the problem?

For most Christians and many other people the Bible is a familiar and dearly-loved book. Psalms, Proverbs, stories of the Patriarchs, the parables of Jesus, inspirational passages in book after book (as in Isaiah, Micah, Romans, and others) and memorable incidents and images spilling off page after page. Individual verses, and often longer passages as well, have been committed to memory, and are resources to comfort, encourage, and inspire. In the memorable words of 2 Timothy 3:16-17, *"All scripture is inspired by God and is useful for teaching, for reproof, for correction, and for training in righteousness, so that everyone who belongs to God may be proficient, equipped for every good work."* When that was written, of course, "all scripture" referred to the Old Testament, none of the writings in our New Testament having yet attained recognition as "scripture."

The word "inspiration" appears in that passage, and has endured in what the church teaches concerning the Bible. Along with that, the passage speaks of the *relevance* of the Bible for the church's teaching of theology and for its instruction in godly living. The content of the Bible is at one level, of course, historical. While not objective history according to the standards of modern historians, it is a significant source – in some cases the only source – of information concerning the history of Israel, the life of Jesus, and the founding of the church. At another level it is pedagogical, that is, teaching material, and that applies to the "historical" passages as well as to books such as Proverbs. In I Corinthians 10, Paul reminds his readers of events from the time of the Exodus and Israel's wilderness years, and then concludes, *"These things happened to them to serve as an example, and they were written down to instruct us, on whom the ends of the ages have come. So if you think you are standing, watch out that you do not fall."*(I Cor. 10:11-12)

Bible Study is a foundational element in both congregational life and personal piety, which serves as evidence of two closely-related realities. One is the recognition of the value of Scripture for the purposes delineated in 2 Timothy. The other is even more immediate; the recognition that there is an existential aspect to the Bible. In passage after passage it seems that we are looking in a mirror. What we experience is not an *old story*, but *our story*. As one example, the prehistory written in Genesis 1-11 can be read most productively not as a literal account of creation and fall, but as a description of the relationship of God to the creation, and the relationship of humans to God, to the rest of creation, and to each other. In the church, the Bible is read and preached as a text in which we are present – a word that addresses *us*. At the time of the Reformation, in a church cut adrift from its authoritarian roots and its center of dogma, the Reformers asserted that the Bible alone, *sola Scriptura*, was the source and norm of its evangelical doctrine.

23

The Bible is not only revered and loved. It is, from any perspective, a quite remarkable book. Its influence on Western culture is unparalleled. It has had a profound influence on the music, art, literature, and law of the Western world. The writing is, itself, an amazing achievement in its variety, scope, and beauty. The diligence with which it has been arranged, edited, interpreted, and preserved is astounding.

As one bit of evidence, consider the work of Old Testament scholar David Noel Freedman.[8] His exhaustive analysis of the Hebrew text and the scrolls on which it was long preserved reveals the awesome diligence with which ancient scholars labored in the formation of the text. In his analysis of word-counts and letter-counts in the Hebrew Bible he has discovered a "precise, built-in symmetry of the whole work." He reports that the first half of the Hebrew Bible, including the Torah and the Former Prophets, contains 149,641 words, and the second half, consisting of the Latter Prophets and the Writings (excluding Daniel, written too late to be a factor in the efforts of those ancient editors who had labored to create the symmetry), contains 149,937 words, a difference of only 296 words. His analysis goes much further, but even this single statistic leaves one in awe of the extraordinary accomplishments of these "men and women moved by the Holy Spirit" (2 Peter 1:21) who brought the text into being.

Beyond the linguistic, statistical, scholarly study of the Bible, one is moved by the hearts that have been touched, the lives changed by encounters with the Bible, and the witness of people who – with whatever words or phrases they have used – declare that they have been drawn to God, touched by the Spirit of God, claimed by Christ, or the like. Whatever else can be said about it (and the coin does have another side), there can be little doubt that the books of the Bible were written as testimony and exhortation to faith, and have inspired and shaped the lives

---

8   Freedman, David Noel. "The Symmetry of the Hebrew Bible." Studia Theologica 46 (1992): pp.83-108

of countless individuals, have called people to faith and have brought forth acts of love and mercy.

But that is only one side of the story. The other side is that the Bible is a difficult and mysterious book. It is a text in which the Spirit of God is present, yet from which the minds and personalities of the human authors are not absent. It was written by a host of different authors, and a majority of it was reworked by editors, over a period of more than 1,000 years, and it contains stories far older. It was written in Hebrew (with a smattering of Aramaic) and Greek, written amid ancient cultures and customs in which government, politics, economic life, and religious practices were different than they are today and differed significantly within the Bible itself.

It has often been maintained by some individuals in both the Jewish and Christian communities that the Bible contains no contradictions or inconsistencies. When such seem to appear, we are told, the problem is not in the text, but in the limited faith, knowledge, or perception of the reader. But to most, even the casual reader, it is clear that the authors bring differing perspectives on a number of issues, sometimes seeming to be – even deliberately – presenting alternative or corrective views. Greatest of all difficulties is the fact that in reading or studying the Bible, our own personalities and our own histories are involved in interaction with what was written by those holy ones of old.

I regard it as a disservice to both the Bible and the faith that in the long history of biblical interpretation the Bible has often been assigned a degree of perfection which the text itself never claims. It has been asserted that the text is not only "inspired," a word which is itself biblical and which I and nearly all Christians accept (though understandings of the term would vary), but "inerrant," and on the basis of that claim the Bible's perfection in all matters, scientific, historical, meteorological, ethical, (and who knows what else) has been asserted.

One result of this approach is that denial of plain evidence in the fields of science and history has become a virtual cottage industry among fundamentalist Christians. Fantastic claims and theories abound concerning Noah's flood, theorizing as to the source of water sufficient to cover the entire earth to the depth of the summit of Ararat (or perhaps Everest?) and further theorizing as to where it went; the story of the "NASA scientist" who supposedly discovered meteorological evidence that the "sun stood still" as described in Joshua 10; attempts to make room for dinosaurs in the Genesis 1 story of creation, and more. The record of such dubious "scholarship" is long, and has served to diminish, rather than increase, respect for the Bible in the general population. It has, in fact, undercut the whole doctrine of "inerrancy." The felt need on the part of some people to fill in what is perceived as lacking in the text by creating elaborate explanations, as in the cases above, would seem to indicate that a corollary of "inerrancy" is "inadequacy."

So, how do we approach the Bible? What is the place of this beloved and difficult book in our lives of faith? The "Statement of Faith" in the Constitution of the Evangelical Lutheran Church in America offers one perspective. It expresses a three-fold understanding of the term "Word of God," declaring – in a deliberately hierarchical order:

"a. Jesus Christ is the Word of God incarnate....

b. The proclamation of God's message to us as both Law and gospel is the Word of God....

c. The canonical Scriptures of the Old and New Testaments are the written Word of God...."

Concerning the Bible, it says, further: *"This church accepts the canonical Scriptures of the Old and New Testaments as the inspired Word of God and the authoritative source and norm of its proclamation, faith, and life."* The Bible is a treasured and irreplaceable witness of faith for faith, but in the Lutheran understanding of the term, it is not the ultimate Word of God. That status is held only by the Christ to whom the Scriptures testify, the one who declared, *"You search the scriptures because you think that in them you have eternal life; and it is they that testify on my behalf.*" (John 5:39)

By way of analogy, some words of St. Paul may be helpful. In speaking of his own ministry (2 Corinthians 12:6), Paul writes that he has refrained from boasting *"so that no one may think better of me than what is seen in me and heard from me."* I would advocate the same humility in the church's approach to reading, studying, teaching, and preaching the Bible. We would do well to remember that in the writing of the New Testament and in the formation of the canon, the doctrine of "inspiration" was *derived from* the church's encounter with those texts and not first *assigned to them.* We know that the writings of the New Testament came to have the status of "Scripture" as the church read and used them and came to recognize them as authentic witnesses to the gospel. The view that they were inspired came via community recognition and affirmation. And the community turned to them for guidance in faith and conduct.

In every time of contention over social issues or "moral values", a principal point of contention concerns "what the Bible says," or in what variety of ways participants in the debate read and interpret the Bible. That is not news, and it does not apply only when social issues or moral values are under discussion. The church wrestled with questions of hermeneutics (the principles of interpretation of texts) even before those writings we know as the New Testament were composed. From discussion of the Gentile mission (Acts 15), to the Arian controversies of the 3rd and 4th Centuries, to the Reformation, to issues of predestination and sexuality, debates concerning hermeneutics have continued. Only presenting issues and cited texts have changed.

The points I will try to make are not new, but sometimes a simple restatement – the same thing said in different words – can help one to think through a question in a new way.

The basic point is deceptively simple, and is a point with which hardly anyone would disagree: each of us reads Scripture through the lenses of our own history, our own personality, our own life experience, and through ways we have learned to approach the Bible. To say that again, and in more debatable terms, we bring to the Bible our own prejudices, and "what the Bible says" (especially when used in argument) is almost never simply what the Bible says.

Every Christian, in encountering Scripture and gospel, is faced with a dual task: what I would define as both *studying the words*, and *learning the music*. The words, of course, are the text of the Bible. The music is the good news of God's love shown in Jesus Christ and conveyed ever anew by the Holy Spirit. Virtually all would agree that the Bible is not a "flat text". Not every word is of equal value or significance. The summary of the reign of King Pekah of Israel (2 Kings 15), to take one example, might be considered as of lesser significance than the parables of Jesus. Not every passage is equally literal in its meaning. Narrative passages, parables, poetry, and obvious metaphors are different types of material, and each presents a different challenge to the reader. In other words, a process of interpretation is necessary to bring portions of the Bible to a teachable, preachable level of understanding. Evidence that this is so is seen in the fact that readers of the Bible – whether laity, Sunday School teachers, pastors, or the most distinguished of scholars and exegetes – so frequently differ in conclusion and application.

The Bible is, as pointed out above, a library; sixty-six writings, covering more than 1000 years of written tradition and centuries, perhaps nearly a millennium, more of oral tradition; written in three languages, in slightly differing cultures and in vastly differing social and political contexts. As others have commented, the wonder is not that parts of it are hard to comprehend, the wonder is that we find so much of it filled with message and meaning for our lives, individually and collectively, today.

The Bible contains a gathering of insights, reports of revelatory events, dialogues and even debates concerning the ways of God. Note, for example, this debate: Exodus declares that God is *"a jealous God, punishing children for the iniquity of parents, to the third and the fourth generations....*" (Exodus 20:5); Deuteronomy 23 specifies that no offspring of an illicit union shall be admitted to the assembly of the LORD *"even to the tenth generation"*; and the story of the Israelites in the wilderness contains the story in which the entire families of the rebels Korah, Dathan, and Abiram are put to death for the sins of those leaders (Numbers 16). But Deuteronomy 24:16 specifies that *"Parents shall not be put to death for their children, nor shall children be put to death for their parents; only for their own crimes may persons be put to death"*. The prophet Ezekiel (18:20) declares, *"A child shall not suffer for the iniquity of a parent, nor a parent suffer for the iniquity of a child; the righteousness of the righteous shall be his own, and the wickedness of the wicked shall be his own"*. And Jeremiah 31:29-30 makes the same point: *"In those days they shall no longer say: 'The parents have eaten sour grapes, and the children's teeth are set on edge.' But all shall die for their own sins; the teeth of everyone who eats sour grapes shall be set on edge."*

Examples could be multiplied. The words of Jesus in the Sermon on the Mount (Matthew, chapters 5-7) are striking. In direct challenge to the teachings of his community and to the words of Scripture, Jesus repeatedly tells his audience, *"You have heard that it was said.... But I say to you."* With those words, Jesus offers correctives and new insights related both to the original meaning of the passages he cites and to the interpretations prevailing in his day.

But, if the Bible does not convey – as a whole and in all of its parts – a consistent, unvarying, faithful word from God; if the Bible contains dialogue, debate, challenge from one writer to another; then how can we rely on it at all? Is there, then, any sense in which the church can claim the Bible as "source and norm," as "authoritative for its faith and life?" Many Christians have lived with what someone has termed a bumper-sticker theology: "God said it. I believe it. That settles it." Most of the rest of us will cite passages on one side of an issue to counteract passages cited on the other side of the issue. Yet, even while doing so, we will object to "proof-texting" and scoff at the idea that issues can be settled simply by adding up passages "pro" and "con."

So, what is this business of biblical authority? Is the Bible the "Word of God", or not? In response, let me make a very humble claim: the Bible bears witness to the "Word of God" and can be accorded that title because in all of it God is the center, the passion, the focus; and the Bible – all of it – as the core witness to God's revelation is therefore the material with which the Spirit works in the church and on our hearts.

A bit of reflection will remind anyone familiar with church history – in some cases with history in general – that through the centuries church and society have chosen to embrace, to amend, or even to ignore parts of Scripture and earlier tradition. Some examples are well-known. In the first century, C.E., the Council of Jerusalem (Acts 15) was driven to reinterpret, or perhaps "re-prioritize" is better, what they had learned from their Scripture and to ignore significant elements which were part of their tradition. Slave-holders in 19th century America defended the institution of slavery on biblical grounds, as did defenders of apartheid in 20th century South Africa.

So let us look at the use of Scripture in the churches today. As one illustration, the relative equality of women and men, including the fitness of women for ordained ministry, is under consideration in only a few denominations. The rest see it as an issue settled by the witness of the Bible. But while some see the Bible as affirming equality and fitness, others argue hierarchy or "orders of creation" and cite the example of Jesus (who chose twelve male disciples) as grounds for barring women from ordained ministry. Denominations which baptize the infant children of Christian parents, and those which baptize "believers" both find support in the New Testament.

In dealing with some issues, as noted above, the church has followed the prioritizing done by Jesus or St. Paul. In other places we make our own choices, either in the way we prioritize passages or in the way we apply them. An obvious example is the way most churches deal with divorce. As reflected in the New Testament, Jewish law permitted a man to give his wife a certificate of divorce and send her away (Matthew 5). Jesus declared that law to be a concession to "hardness of heart", and asserted (Mark 10, Luke 16) that divorce was impermissible, or (Matthew 5) permissible only in cases of "unchastity." St. Paul added one more permissible circumstance, writing that a Christian was not bound to remain in a marriage if abandoned by an unbelieving spouse (I Corinthians 7).

In modern Western societies, nearly 50% of first marriages end in divorce. Many of those divorces are based simply on "irreconcilable differences", very few on the biblically accepted ground of abandonment by an unbelieving spouse, some unknown number on the biblically accepted ground of unchastity. Many churches, perhaps most, frown on divorce, but acknowledge a much longer list of acceptable grounds, notably various forms of abuse. In most churches, divorced persons are not ostracized. Most churches permit the remarriage of those who have been divorced, and even where the church holds to the viewpoint that they are adulterers, their participation in the church is welcomed under the rubric of forgiveness.

So we return to the question: How do we understand the Bible and biblical authority? Some would identify the Bible as in the first place a rule book, in which the most vital passages are *rules for living*: the "Ten Commandments" (with or without the rest of the law codes of the Pentateuch), the Sermon on the Mount, St. Paul's list of household duties, and the book of Proverbs. Others would place the emphasis on what the Bible teaches of *morals and values*: the prophets on justice, Leviticus on purity, Jesus on love for neighbor, and the like. Still others find the center in the *teachings of Jesus*: parables, Sermon on the Mount, wisdom sayings, and teachings on discipleship. And some, of course, regard the Bible as the *authority on all things*, including matters of science and history, leading them to insist that creation was a six-day process, that the sun literally stood still, and that Noah's ark remains atop Ararat. But Lutherans have, in general, sought to affirm with the great reformer, Martin Luther, that what is to be prized most highly is *was Christum treibt* ("what conveys Christ"). Luther was, in fact, willing even to dismiss portions of the Bible which he saw as falling short of that standard.

What I say next is meant quite sincerely. It seems to me that it should be our normal expectation that reading the Bible would be much like any other reading. Apart from what God chooses to do with our encounter with the Bible, we would expect to take from the Bible what we bring to the Bible, with only information and memorable phrasings touching our minds, with poetry and poignant passages touching our hearts. Thus, it is not surprising that a majority of Bible reading, even "Bible Study" serves more to reinforce than to transform. We are drawn to texts that say what we already believe, that affirm convictions long-held.

To illustrate, let us give attention to individual issues and passages, taking brief note of the range of interpretation and application existing within the Christian churches. We might begin by asking again about the place of women in the church. Should women serve in the ordained ministry? Some churches, including the ELCA, answer in the affirmative, citing a host of passages, including Galatians 3 (*"there is no longer male and female"); Genesis 1 ("in the image of God he created them, male and female he created them"); Genesis 2 with its reference to woman as the *ezer* ("ez-AIR", translated "helper"). Of special interest in that passage is the fact that in the rest of the Old Testament the word is used almost exclusively of God as the helper and of humans only when they fail to provide help. Also cited are the references to Prisca/Priscilla (Acts 18), Mary (Romans 16:6), and other women "working in the gospel" or playing other significant roles in the church. Other churches, including the Lutheran Church – Missouri Synod and the Roman Catholic Church, answer in the negative, citing passages referring to woman as *"the weaker vessel"* (I Peter 3) who should *"keep silence in the church"* (I Corinthians 14), noting Jesus' selection of twelve *men* as his inner circle of disciples, and appealing to the structure or "orders" of creation. The diverse answers to the question of the ordination of women illustrate that, even among earnest and knowledgeable Christians, responses are not based simply on "what the Bible says," but also on entrenched church polity, individual life experience, and other factors.

Another prominent theme which illustrates the point is the New Testament view of the relationship of the "Jesus movement" to human authority – to government. The picture is complex. Much traditional commentary sees Jesus as advocating total pacifism (*"if anyone strikes you on the right cheek, turn the other also," etc.)* Matthew 5:38-41. But some recent commentary reads those verses as advocating non-violent resistance in a style later used to advantage by Gandhi and Martin Luther King, Jr. Romans 13 has traditionally been read as advocating "quietism" and conformity with the claims and demands of civil authority, and Acts 5:29 as setting a limit on Christian obedience (*"we must obey God rather than any human authority"*). But do those passages give adequate guidance *vis a vis* our relationship to government as we consider, for example, the somewhat ambiguous saying of Jesus on "God and Caesar"? In other words, just what are we to render to Caesar and to God? And to what degree are real-life political realities and controversies present in the New Testament? For example, what are we to make of the persistent allusions to kingship in the Passion narratives, including the wording on the sign ordered by Pilate, *"Jesus of Nazareth, the King of the Jews"* (John 19:19b)? Additionally, a variety of historical circumstances are reflected in the various New Testament books. Over against the passages seeking to establish a relatively harmonious relationship with civil authority, especially passages from Luke and St. Paul, stands Revelation, in which civil authority (the Roman Empire) is seen as the beast: evil, and to be resisted at all costs. Even in our reading of Romans 13, commentators often fail to note how Paul's statement concerning the role of "the governing authorities" does more than counsel obedience to the authorities "instituted by God." In that passage St. Paul also defines a proper and limited role for civil authority, and offers guidance to help the Christian recognize when and where that authority is – and is not – functioning as a servant of God. The point is that, though the same Bible is referenced, the spectrum of Christian relationship to civil authority ranges from "peace churches," pacifist traditions, and conscientious objection to military service; to churches that are consistently affirmative of, and place a heavy emphasis on, obedience to civil authority; to the "Jesus-as-Rambo" depiction favored by people fascinated by their images of Armageddon. More could be said, but again, the diversity of interpretation shows that our responses are something other than simply "what the Bible says."

And yet one more example: what the New Testament has to say on material wealth. We live in a generally affluent culture. In this culture, the issue of wealth and poverty is a touchy one. Luke, in many ways the best-loved of the Gospels, is clearly an advocate for the poor, and presents the sayings of Jesus on this issue in a form somewhat harsher and thus less welcome to our ears and minds than Matthew. At times our cultural assumptions are in clear conflict with the words of Jesus. In the parable of the Talents (Matthew 25), the hard-nosed nobleman expects at least interest on his money. Elsewhere in Scripture, one believer is forbidden to take interest from another (Deuteronomy 23, Ezekiel 18 & 22). Yet in our economic system, interest on money is a basic factor, something we could not imagine doing without. We cannot give a careful hearing to Luke without becoming aware of a cultural conflict. What do we learn, how do we reflect, how much do we rationalize?

The foregoing is simply an attempt to point out that in the history of the church, as well as in our individual histories, Christians have chosen to embrace, amend, or ignore elements of the biblical tradition. To some degree this is necessary; we must concede the truth of the statement that "you can prove anything from the Bible," but with a caveat. You can prove anything from the Bible if you are willing to "flatten the text" and use the Bible in that way. The Bible does say that, in some cases, when a city is conquered, the conquerors are to let nothing that breathes remain alive (Deuteronomy 20). The Bible does contain passages that approve (or seem to approve) of slavery, patriarchy, misogyny, cheating, abuse, cruelty, prejudice of many sorts, hatred, violence, war, and genocide; and to present a god (lower case intentional) who is at times harsh, capricious, and vengeful.

But one significant point I wish to make is that the Bible is not a flat text. It is "Word of God" not in the sense of dictation or direct quote. The Bible did not fall from heaven, but was written by human authors who were in some way moved by the Spirit. Further, they were human authors from whom human culture, sensibility, and opinion had not been erased. It is my contention (and I know some will disagree, even vehemently) that part of the difficult, risky, often subjective, but inescapable task of Bible study (whether by the most or least learned reader) is to discern where and how human culture, sensibility, and opinion are present in and behind the text.

We might cite examples. It is possible to read Paul's advice that women should keep silence in the church as reflecting his desire that Christians live with some respect for the culture in which they live, so as not to cause offense or appear to their neighbors to be weird. If we consider it in that light, we might choose to agree or disagree with Paul's missionary sensibilities, but his judgment would be one growing out of and applying to his time and culture. In the Old Testament, laws and customs upholding patriarchy need not be read as God's "everywhere and always" will for humankind, but as reflecting the culture of the people in whom faith was at that time vibrantly alive or, in some cases, struggling to survive. As I read the biblical prescriptions for conquest of the Promised Land, and the command mentioned above that in some cases the conquerors were to let nothing that breathed remain alive, I find that so at variance with many other portions of the Bible that I read it not as an authentic word from the Lord but as reflecting the understandings, historical circumstances, religious passions, and patterns of warfare prevailing at that time and in the cultural milieu of which Israel was a part.

Does that mean I become a judge of the biblical text? The word, "judge" may make you uneasy; but if the question is whether I make *judgments* as I read, the answer is, obviously, "Yes." That answer is unavoidable. And for you as well, it is inescapable. Whatever your understanding of the text; the nature of the text; and its relationship to you, to the church, and to the world, you bring your perception and judgment to the text. To answer "No," to deny your subjective involvement in the process of reading and interpreting is, in fact, dangerous. In every encounter with the Bible, *you are there!* Somehow, as you read, your mind is at work discerning whether a phrase is literal or metaphorical, making decisions in regard to meaning. "Surely", your mind tells you, "'Ephraim is a cake not turned' (Hosea 7:8) cannot mean that the tribe of Ephraim is actually, literally, an unturned pancake. It is, it *must be* the case that the tribe of Ephraim is acting in an unwise, *half-baked* manner" (to use a more modern term). And at times you recognize the voice of the author. You recognize Paul's words in Galatians 5:12 – "I wish those who unsettle you would castrate themselves" – to be a statement of Paul's exasperation rather than an expression of the Spirit's yearning!

Even the famous words of advice for studying the Bible ("First apply yourself totally to the text, then apply the text totally to yourself") recognize the need for careful study and discernment before one is ready to apply the text. Such study and discernment is required because there is no word of Scripture that is not culturally conditioned. Numerous examples have already been cited, but probably the most persuasive evidence is to be found in the way we read, quote, and use the Bible. In the early part of this chapter, it is asserted that the Bible is a familiar and dearly-loved book, that individual verses have been committed to memory as resources to comfort, encourage, and inspire. Mention was made of our love for Psalms, Proverbs, stories of the Patriarchs, parables of Jesus, and inspirational passages found elsewhere. But there are other books and passages seldom read, memorized, or used as sermon texts.

The issue is not New Testament versus Old; in fact, a majority of those familiar and loved passages are probably to be found in the Old Testament. I am convinced the issue is culture. In some respects the New Testament has an advantage, because Greek culture, Greek language, and Roman administration and law are more clearly in our line of cultural ancestry than the Semitic world of the Old Testament. But the margin is not large. It is rather the case that in Old Testament and New alike, "everyone loves a good story," and each Testament contains a goodly number of good stories. Further we can most easily read and assimilate passages that deal with universal – less culture-bound – human experience and emotion. Joy and sorrow, pain and fear, awe and reverence, delight and pathos are pretty much alike in every human heart and culture. Words of comfort and promise, peace and reassurance, words that challenge and call out the best in us, resonate in human minds and hearts. And the varied topics and situations found in Jesus' parables are familiar in most human societies and relationships.

On the other hand, the portions of Scripture least read are those most culture-bound. The extensive law-codes of the Pentateuch have proven an insurmountable obstacle to many who set out to read the Bible from cover to cover. Details of tabernacle and temple dimensions and construction have served as antidotes to insomnia. Details of covenant ceremonies, laws of levirate marriage, genealogies and other "list" passages attract only scholars or potential "Bible Bowl" contestants. For many of us, the distinction between the whole Bible and our individual, congregational, and denominational Bibles – *abridged* Bibles – is found in this matter of culture.

One inevitable result is that many of the areas of controversy within the Christian family, whether within or between denominations, relate to disagreement or uncertainty as to whether (and to what degree) given passages reflect older cultures or reflect God's own authentic and eternal principles and ideals. In situations already mentioned: slavery, sexuality, gender equality, war, economics, divorce – the most significant disagreements concern understandings of Scripture at this basic level.

But the most significant point I wish to make is to express confidence in the work of the Holy Spirit. The Holy Spirit teaches – wills to teach – the church. That is the promise of Jesus in the farewell discourses in the Gospel of John (14:26). It is affirmed in Luther's Small Catechism that the Spirit "calls, gathers, enlightens, and sanctifies" the church. That most emphatically does not mean that the church always gets it right. Luther's insistence that "Popes and Councils can err" applies with equal validity to every Christian individual and collective in history, and is the cause of much frustration and some near-despair. The people who get it right (Athanasius, for one example) may face hardship and hostility rather than affirmation. Individuals, congregations, and denominations may continue to be wrong for generations, even centuries. Ultimately, I suppose, there can be no assurance that the church will ever get it right. It is our conviction, after all, that we are saved by grace alone. My confidence, therefore, is a matter of faith in the ultimate triumph of God.

However, I find it striking that as the "ever-reforming" church has moved through history and faced new issues, it has not been prompted to depart from the Bible, but to move instead to new perceptions and deeper understandings of Scripture. Here too, of course, new understandings and novel insights need careful and prayerful review within the community of scholarship and the family of faith. But I am convinced that the Spirit has guided and taught the church, opening the eyes of faith to new understandings faithful to the living Christ, by speaking through the Scriptures in powerful ways at critical times. The era of creedal development was one such time, the Reformation era was another; the struggles over the issues of slavery, and later human rights issues including the struggle for Civil Rights in the USA and against apartheid in South Africa, were still others; the place of women (including the question of ordination) still another. Efforts of the various denominations to produce social statements, a process of ecclesiastical discernment in which members are challenged to be involved in prayer and study, is an ongoing plea for the Spirit's guidance.

In the heat of the slavery controversy in the 19th Century, it seemed that the slave-holders had a greater claim on biblical authority, but today most Christians recognize that the entire message of the gospel is more persuasive than any listing of texts. In considering the place of women, once the question is asked, new insights emerge. *"So God created humankind in his image, in the image of God he created them, male and female he created them"* (Genesis 1:27) clearly states that male and female are equal, and equally in God's image, a point that was not clearly perceived for centuries – not until the Spirit opened the eyes of those ready to receive new insight from an old text.

Today, in many minds and hearts across the church, there is a conviction that the Spirit has opened eyes to new understandings and a new welcome for faithful sisters and brothers who differ only in sexual orientation or gender identity. That is the topic of this book, as it is a question before the churches, including the ELCA. As we proceed, we will continue to think, pray, and study to learn both the biblical words and the gospel music.

Chapter 3
Scripture and Sexuality

So we turn to the Bible, looking at the verses most frequently quoted in discussion of homosexuality, thinking together about whether and how those passages are relevant, and then thinking about how those parts relate to the whole of Scripture. And that means asking *how* (and, of course, *whether*) we read the Bible.

It is certainly true that Christians read the Bible in a variety of ways. Some are more drawn to a literal reading, others to historical-critical approaches. Some are more inclined to see Scripture as a guide-book or law-book, others lean toward interpretations in which biblical prescriptions and proscriptions are read in tandem with contemporary research in the social sciences. Some lean on what they see as "the plain meaning" of verses and passages, others relate texts to contexts large or small. In my treatment of biblical texts, it will become clear that I inquire into the basis, the rationale which lies behind the text.

In asking about the relevance of Scripture to the discussion of homosexuality, there are at least two dimensions, two perspectives on Scripture, to be considered. The one which has received the most attention is based on a short list of passages dealing with behaviors to which we would apply the term "homosexual." These passages are found chiefly in the law codes of the Old Testament and in "vice lists" in the New Testament. We will first address the interpretation of these passages. The other perspective, which reads the Bible in a more holistic way, will be presented later.

I learned in seminary that Old Testament laws can be divided into two types: apodictic and casuistic. Apodictic, I was taught, is a term referring to absolutes. "You shall. . . " and "You shall not . . .," without quibbling or qualification. Casuistic meant "case law." It was expressed in terms of "if...then," or "when these circumstances prevail, this is what should be done." The Ten Commandments were specific, declarative, apodictic.

Long before I learned those terms, I was taught in confirmation classes and learned from sermons that the Ten Commandments, "apodictic" in form, were nonetheless sensible, logical, had specific purpose and value in terms of human life and relationships. Even the apodictic laws were not simply arbitrary, as if proceeding from the mind of God and not accessible to human understanding. For example, the apodictic law, "You shall not steal" clearly had practical value in preserving people from fear, loss, suspicion, and violence. And so it was with the rest. Honoring the Sabbath could be understood both in terms of the need for rest, as expressed in Exodus and Deuteronomy, and in terms of the value of giving attention to the Word, as expressed by Martin Luther in his *Small Catechism*.

In our allegiance to the Scriptures, it is appropriate – has always been seen as appropriate – to inquire into the ground and rationale of biblical prohibitions. Most Christians eat meat, including pork (and the "Easter ham"), even though the eating of pork is forbidden in the Old Testament and horrifies our Jewish neighbors. We respond on several bases. In the simplest terms we may quote St. Paul on Christian freedom from the law. When we are asked for clarification, we explain that those prohibitions are based on definitions of "clean" and "unclean" as defined in Old Testament law codes. In addition, and bringing in a "not from the Bible" rationale, the argument has been advanced that some of the prohibitions may have been based on health concerns such as the trichinosis sometimes found in pork.

My point is that it is appropriate for us to seek understanding of biblical law by asking, "What is at stake here?" What were the values being preserved, the dangers or pitfalls avoided by the making and enforcing of this law? How did the biblical writers, whom we believe to have been inspired by God, see the world and the faith as they recorded the moral and ethical concerns to be found in their writings? Why does the Bible say what it says? As previously noted, the bumper sticker approach: *"God said it. I believe it. That settles it."* hardly reflects the Lutheran approach to Scripture. The Lutheran approach, as I have long understood it, involves a passion to inquire, to seek understanding, to invoke the Spirit's guidance as we explore and wrestle with texts, believing that in the process we may encounter the living God.

What is in the Scripture? It is not difficult to read the text, but how do we use Scripture? Why do we accept and follow some biblical injunctions and not others? Sometimes we appeal to the New Testament, but not always. To illustrate: On the one hand, in the ministry of Jesus the status of women is elevated, and the words of St. Paul include the breathtaking declaration that there is no longer male and female. On the other hand, the words of Jesus on divorce are more restrictive than those of Moses. In some areas there is no discernible difference between Old and New.

In the above, the point is to invite us to ask ourselves how we approach and interpret the Bible. Do we understand our own bases of interpretation? Do we let Scripture interpret Scripture by inquiring into the standards and rationale lying behind the Bible's own statements? I know one scholar who uses a principle referred to as "freedom of the text," but which very often sounds suspiciously like "freedom from the context." How do we inquire into the context of biblical law?

All of which is relevant to the current discussions of sexuality, and specifically of homosexuality.

The Bible contains a fairly long list of references to sexuality and sexual behaviors. Concerns regarding incest are there, guidance for those asked to render judgment in cases of rape, statutes based on male "control" of female relatives, and verses dealing with same-sex sexual contact. As is true of the illustrations used above, church and society today accept some, reject some, reinterpret some. To give just one example, few people in Western society today would seriously advocate imposing the death penalty for adultery.

Analysis and Commentary – Old Testament Texts

The most relevant, and most frequently referenced, texts in the Old Testament dealing with "homosexual" activity are in the story of Lot's visitors in Genesis 19, the story of the Levite's concubine in Judges 19, and in the "Holiness Code" of Leviticus (18:22, 20:13). New Testament texts most cited are in the "God gave them up" section of Romans (1:26-28), and in "vice lists" in I Corinthians (6:9-10) and I Timothy (1:9-10). They have this in common: acts that we would term "homosexual" (the appearance of the word in some translations of the Bible is an anachronism) are specifically condemned or are included in lists of vices. I would maintain that all are rooted to some extent in Hebrew/Jewish law. The Leviticus references are part of the law codes, the New Testament references are written by people whose own roots are in that law and culture. They differ in that the Old Testament context includes the practices of Canaanite Baalism and of other neighboring peoples and religions, and the New Testament context includes Greco-Roman culture and the social and religious practices which were part of it. We will look at the New Testament passages in more detail later.

The first two passages cited above are hardly relevant to the discussion. Though the mobs apparently intend to commit same-sex rape, it does not occur. Both texts involve inhospitality, actual or intended violence, desire to dominate and humiliate, and in Judges, *heterosexual* rape. In other biblical references to those stories, only Jude speaks of the sin of Sodom as concerning sexual immorality.

In Leviticus, male-to-male sexual relations are termed "an abomination." (Lev. 18 and 20, NRSV uses the term "abhorrent") The Hebrew word is transliterated *toebah*. It occurs 25 times in the Pentateuch and (by my count) some 87 times in other Old Testament books. Restricting ourselves to the Pentateuch, we find it said that some things are abhorrent to Egyptians, e.g., eating with Hebrews; all shepherds; and Hebrew sacrifices.

Within Israel, the list of abhorrent things includes various sexual practices regarded as incestuous; the sacrificing of children to Molech; male-to-male sex acts; the precious metals which are part of the statues of idols; unspecified things done in the course of idol worship; enticing people to worship other gods; sacrificing an animal that has a defect; idolatry; divination, sorcery, and the like; idolatry (mentioned again as the basis for the command to annihilate other peoples); a woman putting on man's apparel or a man putting on women's apparel; bringing as an offering money gained from prostitution; remarrying a former spouse who has been married to another in the interval; using dishonest weights and measures; and making or casting an idol. Finally, in Deuteronomy 32, a poetic passage declares that the descendants of Jacob have done abhorrent things – again, in context, probably a reference to idolatry.

What shall we say of a list which ranges from child sacrifice to cross-dressing, from incest to the remarriage prohibition, from encouraging idolatry to dishonesty, from sacrificing an imperfect animal to making or casting idols – and which, by the way, gives approval to the total annihilation of other peoples? In chapter 20 of Leviticus, the section which prescribes the death penalty for male-to-male sex also prescribes the death penalty for cursing parents and for adultery, and says that the penalty for sexual relations during a woman's menstruation is that both man and woman are to be "cut off from their people." And Deuteronomy 22:22 adds a death penalty for adultery: "If a man is caught lying with the wife of another man, both of them shall die."

My questions as I approach these texts are the same questions I ask about all other passages. What is conveyed here, for what purpose and against what background? The Leviticus passages, as stated above, are part of a law code. Why are they there? What is the rationale? What is being protected? What is perceived as evil? Or is the evil thought to be so self-evident as to need no elaboration? For some at that time, and for some today, that may be the case simply because of what someone has termed the "gross-out factor" as heterosexuals conjure up images of homosexual acts. But others raise the question: Are we bound to accept as evil everything identified as evil in Scripture, or are we free to inquire, perhaps to disagree, here as elsewhere?

It seems (not only to me) that the various "sexuality" commands and prohibitions in the Old Testament codes are based on a constellation of Israelite concerns, among them:

(a) concern to build and maintain the nation and the family lines within it;
(b) opposition to the influence of neighboring religions;
(c) taboos regarding incest and blood;
(d) preservation of, and respect for, the property rights of men;
(e) respect for Israelite persons and opposition to violence against them; and
(f) the argument from creation which involves the concept of "uncleanness," opposing and regarding as "unclean" anything which seems to violate categories or involves the mixing of categories.

The concern to build and maintain the nation and family lines is prominent in a number of passages. It is the purpose of levirate marriage (Deuteronomy 25:5-6), which specifies that it was the duty of a brother of a deceased man who had died childless to take the dead man's wife so that she might have children who would then be regarded as the children of the dead man, thus preserving the family line. The sin of Onan (Genesis 38:6-10) was not masturbation in any general sense, but was specifically his refusal to fulfill this fraternal obligation. The concern appears also in Naomi's words to Ruth (Ruth 1:12-13), and in the test case presented to Jesus in Matthew 22:24-28. The same concern is certainly present as one element in the prohibition of a man "lying with a man." It is "wasting the seed."

Most of the other concerns are obvious in innumerable texts, but the final one, involving the concept of uncleanness, invites some explanation. The Hebrew Scriptures define the categories of "clean" and "unclean" and provide abundant specific examples. Analysis of the lists reveals that the categories are largely based on what we might call "appropriate" and "inappropriate"; or "proper" and "improper." Animals which have cloven hooves but do not chew the cud (pigs being the notable illustration) are unclean; that is, a proper cloven-hoofed animal should be expected to chew the cud. Sea creatures which do not have scales, such as eels or catfish, are unclean; a proper fish has scales. Birds which do not fly, such as the ostrich, are unclean; a proper bird is capable of flight. Examples could be multiplied: unclean are predators and carrion-eaters; mammals without hooves (Leviticus 11 and related passages), etc. One comic strip pictured God addressing the angels of the "CREATION DESIGN DEPT.," saying to them, "About the penguin – did you not get the 'fish gotta swim, birds gotta fly' memo?"[9]

Of the Israelite concerns in the above list, (c), (e), and (f) may be the most relevant to this discussion. Both church and society are opposed to violence (category "e") in sexual relationships. But that is true of heterosexual as well as homosexual relationships. We are left, then, with two of the categories: taboo and the argument

---

9   Thaves, Bob. Frank and Ernest, Herald Journal (Logan, UT). 25 April 2002, distributed by NEA, Inc.

from creation, which also involves the concept of uncleanness. To which I would add a third not specifically found in Scripture: the often-heard assumption that homosexuality equals promiscuity, a series of wanton, casual and uncommitted sexual liaisons.

Each individual would have to give a personal answer as which is the greater factor. Certainly for some heterosexuals, the taboo is the stronger. These have a strong antipathy, abhorrence, a simply visceral reaction against homosexual orientation and behavior. Others react against the stated agenda of some of the most militant within the gay and lesbian community. Still others, when they see the inclusion of the term "bisexual" in the "sexual orientation" list, misunderstand it as a desire to have all varieties of promiscuity accepted. This is the "not from Scripture" concern. But I know many in the LGBTQ community who are part of the church, and who hold the same convictions and yearnings regarding faithful, committed relationships as we assume to be held by heterosexual Christians. And let it be noted, as mentioned in Chapter 1, that our society is pervasively bombarded with the message that promiscuity is to be accepted if not expected in heterosexual behavior.

Which brings me to the argument from creation. This argument is stated in two forms, outlined in the previous chapter, which I termed "diversity" and "flaw." The diversity point of view asserts that homosexuality is an evidence of diversity in creation. A cursory look in any direction tells us that God delights in diversity. The creation includes roses and tulips; apples, oranges, and coconuts; oak trees and cedars; hummingbirds and ostriches. And persons with diverse sexual orientations and gender identities. It has been reported that behaviors we would classify as homosexual occur in other species in roughly the same proportion as in humans, indicating that the "diversity" point of view cannot be lightly dismissed.

But there is another form of the argument. Here it is asserted that divine intention can be discerned in the fact that we were created male and female, with anatomy designed for intercourse in the interest of propagation of the species. With this basic assertion I have no quarrel. Reproduction is a function shared by all life forms. Reproduction can be identified as a "drive" of all animate and sentient life forms. But in human relationships, sexual activity can be more than that. It functions also as a way to express love, companionship, and intimacy, and as a profound form of communication.

If propagation of the species is the only rationale on which sexual activity is to be permitted, that is very bad news for people such as my wife and I, now past the age of child-bearing. It directs at least a stern "tut-tut" at couples practicing birth control. And, presumably, infertile couples are to cease and desist once their condition is fully diagnosed. In reality, most adults in the western world – but not all – would expand their view of acceptable sexual activity to include intercourse which is not aimed at procreation, such as mentioned above.

Humor aside, if the argument is accepted that "biology is destiny," it is clear that homosexuality is not according to divine intention. One could term it a quirk, a flaw, an imperfection. As noted above, some biologists report that homosexuality is not a strictly human phenomenon, but that a small percentage of creatures within other species also exhibit behaviors we would call homosexual. Thus, if we do not accept the "diversity" position, it would seem that we must place homosexuality in the category Christians might term "fallen creation." Let me say in the interest of clarity that my position wanders between "diversity" and "flaw." But at the moment I wish to focus on the "flaw" position.

I am nearsighted. My brother was diagnosed with juvenile-onset diabetes at the age of 13. A friend named Cynthia has lupus. Some of us have allergies, others depression. Some have learning disabilities or developmental disabilities of various kinds. The list could be immensely expanded. All living things in creation are subject to many conditions which we regard as not in accord with divine intention. Many, if not most (if not all) of us are not in accord with perfect design. But one thing that the items on the above list have in common is that they are unchosen. They are simply part of who we are. While theologically they may serve as evidence of a fallen creation, we can understand them to be part of our human burden in a creation corrupted by sin, and not part of our sinful human rebellion. In the church we assume that such imperfections are part of our common humanity, even as we accept and embrace one another in love.

In summary, when the four Old Testament passages are read with a concern for consistency, and with sensitivity to the cultural context, none would seem to be relevant to the current discussion of sexual orientation and committed same-gender relationships.

Analysis and Commentary – New Testament Texts

We turn now to the New Testament references. As mentioned above, the New Testament contains "vice lists" in I Corinthians 6:9-11, I Timothy 1:10, and other places – lists of vices which are said to exclude people from the kingdom of God. We will look at them now and return to them later. Included in the list are drunkenness, greed, reviling, and thievery along with two words which are generally taken to refer to male behaviors we would term homosexual. There is some uncertainty as to how the Greek words are to be translated. One of them may refer to male prostitution or to the Roman practice of pederasty. The other combines words for "male" and "intercourse." In some translations it appears as "sodomite" or "homosexual."[10] Whatever the precise meaning, it is clear that the words refer to male behaviors *we* would term in some sense "homosexual." But we should be wary as to how we use the vice lists. The modern world understands alcoholism somewhat differently than the first century viewed "drunkenness," and many in our culture would be reluctant to

---

10 The translation and interpretation of the Greek terms is based on the analysis of Dr. Ed. Miller.

49

assume that people who accumulate great wealth are excluded from the kingdom.

The strongest passage, and to many the clearest, in the New Testament opposing same-sex sexual activity is Romans 1:26-28, which declares: *"For this reason, God gave them up to degrading passions. Their women exchanged natural intercourse for unnatural, and in the same way also the men, giving up natural intercourse with women, were consumed with passion for one another. Men committed shameless acts with men and received in their own persons the due penalty for their error."*

Several things must be said about this passage. There is no denying the content. But there should also be no neglect of the context. The passage appears as part of a long argument in which St. Paul makes the point that all have sinned, and that every mouth which might be tempted to claim merit before God should be stopped. Beware! In its context this statement is part of a set-up, a trap not unlike the early section of Amos (1:3 - 2:16) in which the Israelite reader, approving the condemnations of Damascus, Philistia, Tyre, Edom, the Ammonites, Moab, and Judah, winds up condemning self.

Here in Romans, those under the law (Jews) and those outside the law (Gentiles) are said to stand alike under God's judgment, leading to the verdict, *"so that every mouth may be silenced and the whole world may be held accountable to God. For 'no human being will be justified in his sight' by deeds prescribed by the law."* And after the verdict comes the punch-line, the incredible message of justification by grace alone through faith alone as a gift: *"But now, apart from law, the righteousness of God has been disclosed, and is attested by the law and the prophets, the righteousness of God through faith in Jesus Christ for all who believe. For there is no distinction, since all have sinned and fall short of the glory of God; they are now justified by his grace as a gift, through the redemption that is in Christ Jesus, whom God put forward as a sacrifice of atonement by his blood, effective through faith."*

It would seem abundantly clear in Paul's argument that the grace of God, which comes as a gift and is sufficient to justify all (and that means all of us) who are described as standing under God's condemnation apart from the blood of Jesus, is sufficient to justify also this part of humanity – those who are not heterosexual – who come in faith and place their trust and hope in that same gift of grace. Or are we to maintain that they (one example among others in Paul's three-chapter recital of the sins of humanity) are sinners beyond other sinners and beyond the reach of grace? Or would any maintain that non-heterosexuals, even those in committed relationships, move away from any claim on God's grace because they continue in their sexual practices, thus indicating "imperfect repentance"? But if that is the case, what of the rest of us? Do we not continue, sometimes for a lifetime, to struggle with our own specific and abiding issues, sins, and temptations? Can any among us claim that we, week by week, forsake the sins of the past once we have confessed them and heard the word of absolution, and find only new and original sins each week?

There is more to be said. Paul's specific words in Romans 1:26-27 deserve special attention. As noted above, there is no question that St. Paul itemizes practices we would term homosexual as a dreadful example of human degradation and perversity (though we should again remember that it is included in a long passage which makes the point that *no one* is justified except by God's grace as a gift which is ours through faith in Jesus Christ). But I am particularly interested in the references to "natural" and "unnatural." Two meanings or applications are possible. The less probable of the two is that St. Paul is referring to what is "natural" for the persons involved. The statements that women "*exchanged* ..." or men were "*giving up* natural intercourse ..." might point in this direction. If we choose this option, Paul's argument is that these individuals are acting against their own inclinations (what we would term "orientation"), which Paul assumes to be heterosexual.

I consider it more probable that St. Paul uses the terms "natural" and "unnatural" in reference to the "argument from creation" or "natural law," described above. This view is supported by the fact that in this long passage in Romans, St. Paul asserts the condemnation of Jews on the basis of the law, and the condemnation of Gentiles on the basis of the *"law written on their hearts,"* making specific reference to creation in his statement that *"what can be known about God is plain to them, because God has shown it to them. Ever since the creation of the world his eternal power and divine nature, invisible though they are, have been understood and seen through the things he has made."* (Rom. 1:19-20)

But the argument from creation must be used with caution. For one thing, Paul uses the same vocabulary in his "wild olive shoot" analogy in Romans 11, where he declares that it is unnatural for Gentiles to be included among God's people, describing them as unnatural grafts – the *wild shoot grafted in* (something no olive-grower would do!) where the natural branches were broken off. Furthermore, natural law has been used as an argument by those who defended segregation in the U.S. and apartheid in South Africa, among other and even worse examples. Natural law is part of the argument still used by some to defend their opposition to the full equality of women. And, if we wish to base an argument on creation, we must ask if, in fact, observation and research support the argument.

In the discussion of homosexuality, what is known of the pre-scientific world of the Old Testament and of the first century reveals no awareness of "homosexual" behaviors in the animal kingdom, or any widespread awareness that a small percentage of humans are oriented in their sexual attractions to members of their own sex. There are terms for those who participate in sexual activity *we* would term homosexual, and a few texts from the ancient world written by persons who are puzzled or troubled by their awareness that they are unlike others, that their proclivities are outside the norm, but to my knowledge none define themselves as simply belonging to a category recognized as homosexual. Use of that term to describe sexual orientation is of relatively recent origin. So far as I am aware, the references to "homosexual" behavior and the writings of the few "homosexual" persons who have left us any documentation simply accepted the judgment of their day that their sexual tendencies were "unnatural."

A Broader Biblical Perspective

At the outset, I stated that there are two perspectives to be considered. To this point, I have permitted those most uncomfortable with the issue of homosexuality to set the agenda, giving attention to the various laws and prohibitions often quoted as militating against full acceptance of homosexuals. But I turn now to the other perspective.

In the current process of study, discernment, and conversation taking place within the ELCA and other churches, I am puzzled that we draw on so limited a selection of biblical texts. Far too much of the conversation is restricted to the short list of biblical texts with which we have dealt to this point, often the "significant seven" from Genesis, Judges, Leviticus, Romans, I Corinthians, and I Timothy. Some would expand that list by moving from exegesis to eisegesis, citing every passage dealing with marriage and all approved heterosexual relationships, including Jesus' sayings on divorce. I would suggest that other texts are fully as germane to this discussion as "the seven" or, for that matter, the texts that identify marriage as a good thing.

Let us, then, turn to other texts and to another way of reading, dare I say "prioritizing," Scripture. My training and experience as a Lutheran pastor and theologian prompt me to see other passages of Scripture as entirely relevant to our current discussion.

In Genesis 2, God declares, *"It is not good that the man should be alone."* It is often maintained by those most opposed to homosexuality that "aloneness" is indeed the appropriate status of persons who are not heterosexual.

Aloneness as the appropriate status of non-heterosexual persons has also been the policy of the ELCA and other denominations in regard to ordination, which can be summed up, "faithfulness in marriage, celibacy in singleness" – and, by the way, the marriage option is available only to heterosexuals. But do not both our theology (read the Lutheran Confessions) and our flesh-and-blood human nature maintain that we are made for relationship? It is a touching detail of the Genesis account that God first attempts to satisfy the man's need for relationship by creating animals. But that is not enough, and woman is created.

But I would assert that Genesis 2 conveys more than simply man-and-woman-to-be-fruitful. I read it as expressing the deep human yearning for intimacy. I will readily concede that too much human "intimacy" is shallow and transient, but I see that to be true of physical relationships between heterosexuals as well as homosexuals.

In our culture, views of marriage relationships may be shaped primarily by the Roman Catholic "sacramental view" of marriage, the Ephesians "Christ and the church" imagery, and by popular sentimentality, expressed in greeting card language. But in I Corinthians 7, St. Paul offers another perspective. He recognizes that not all are made for celibacy, then goes on to refer to marriage as a simple human and practical arrangement to limit sexual immorality. He advises marriage as a way to bring a degree of control when "passions are strong", an estate better than to be "aflame with passion." Not surprisingly, Martin Luther could also speak of marriage from both perspectives. St. Paul's earthy, practical advice, including choice of language, may not reflect the understanding of marriage most dear to us, but it is there! And I would take that as applying equally to heterosexual and homosexual individuals, since all alike share flesh and blood. Unless we would seriously wish to deny humanity to homosexuals, it would seem we should take seriously the teaching of St. Paul and the Lutheran Confessions on the matter of sexuality, the recognition that sexuality, passion, is part of human nature.

Three of the New Testament passages I regard as most significant are from the book of Acts. The first is the commission given to the disciples/apostles that sent them beyond the bounds of their own ethnicity and religious heritage, *"You will be my witnesses in Jerusalem, in all Judea and Samaria, and to the ends of the earth."* (Acts 1:8b) The second is the account of Peter's encounter with Cornelius (the "Conversion of Peter"), including the vision in which Peter is commanded, *"What God has made clean, you must not call profane."* (Acts 10:15b) The third is the Council of Jerusalem (Acts 15), at which God opens the hearts of "Chosen-People-Jews" to see that God's grace and Spirit have run far ahead of their understandings and prejudices. In each of those passages the Spirit leads or pushes the church to see past old divisions and proscriptions, and to leave behind some of the "clean/unclean" categories from their older traditions. Might it be time for us to leave old prejudices behind?

And there is more. In the Gospel of John, Jesus gives *one* command to his new community, *"I give you a new commandment, that you love one another."* (John 13:34a). *One* commandment? Is this to be read as the *sole* commandment given by Jesus in John's presentation of the gospel, or simply as the *preeminent* commandment? In either case, it is relevant to our current discussion.

Referring back to the "flaw" discussion on an earlier page, why do we not discuss St. Paul's cosmic understanding of the fall of humanity into sin, as in Romans 8:18-23, which speaks of the groaning of the fallen creation? There we are reminded of God's anguish over the struggles, burdens, and divisions that exist anywhere in the created order.

Mention was made earlier of the "vice lists" found in I Corinthians 6:9-10 and I Timothy 1:9-10. In his commentary on Galatians 5:19-21 (the "works of the flesh" passage), Dr.

Ragnar Bring[11] cites other such lists in the New Testament: Romans 13:13; I Corinthians 5:10-11; Ephesians 4:31; 5:3-4; Colossians 3:5,8. All are relevant to the discussion, but I would call your attention to the list of "works of the flesh" cited above. It is part of a passage pleading for love and solidarity within the Christian community. Though it starts with *"fornication, impurity, licentiousness...,"* a reading of the entire list makes it clear that Paul's focus is on conduct that breaks community, including *"enmities, strife, jealousy, anger, quarrels, dissensions, factions...."* The point is that the "vice lists" could – and perhaps should – be turned in the opposite direction. Rather than being used against LGBTQ members, they should be seen as a critique of loveless and judgmental attitudes. The lists stand in the New Testament as evidence of God's passion for inclusion, love, mutual respect, and harmony in the human family and most especially in the church.

Finally, let us move to Paul's breathtaking restatements of the commandments in Romans 13:8-10 and Galatians 5:13-15. Both passages can be read as restatements and expansions of the words of Jesus in the Gospel of John concerning the "new commandment". In both passages Paul affirms love as the fulfilling of the law: "Love does no wrong to a neighbor, therefore love is the fulfilling of the law." To be sure, defining what does "wrong to a neighbor" can be tricky business, but it certainly cannot mean that my neighbor is "wronging me" by any action that bothers or offends me. To venture out on a fairly solid and substantial limb, I think the rubric of doing "wrong to a neighbor" can easily be understood to proscribe incest, pedophilia, promiscuity, abusive behavior, and the like. It cannot easily be wielded against relationships of love and faithfulness between persons who are not heterosexual.

---

11 Bring, Ragnar, <u>Commentary on Galatians</u>. Philadelphia: Muhlenberg Press, 1961. pp. 256-259

Chapter 4
What's an "Abomination"?

I introduce this chapter with an extended quote. This document came into my hands as a forwarded e-mail purportedly addressed to a public figure.[12] I have made minor editorial changes to make it better serve my purpose. It invites reflection on the issues with which we are engaged.

I need some advice from you regarding some elements of God's Laws and how to follow them.

1. *Leviticus 25:44 states that I may possess slaves, both male and female, provided they are purchased from neighboring nations. A friend of mine claims that this applies to Mexicans, but not Canadians. Can you clarify? Why can't I own Canadians?*
2. *I would like to sell my daughter into slavery, as sanctioned in Exodus 21:7. In this day and age, what do you think would be a fair price for her?*

---

12 I am making the assumption that because of the form in which it was transmitted to me, this e-mail has not been copyrighted. If this assumption is erroneous, please inform me, and I would be happy to add authorship information.

3. *1 know that I am allowed no contact with a woman while she is in her period of menstrual uncleanness (Lev. 15:19-24). The problem is how do I tell? I have tried asking, but most women take offense.*

4. *When I burn a bull on the altar as a sacrifice, I know it creates a pleasing odor for the Lord (Lev. 1:9). The problem is my neighbors. They claim the odor is not pleasing to them. Should I smite them?*

5. *I have a neighbor who insists on working on the Sabbath. Exodus 35:2 clearly states he should be put to death. Am I morally obligated to kill him myself, or should I ask the police to do it?*

6. *A friend of mine feels that even though eating shellfish is an abomination (Lev. 11:10), it is a lesser abomination than homosexuality. I don't agree. Can you settle this? Are there 'degrees' of abomination?*

7. *Lev.21:20 states that I may not approach the altar of God if I have a defect in my sight. I have to admit that I wear reading glasses. Does my vision have to be 20/20, or is there some wiggle-room here?*

8. *Most of my male friends get their hair trimmed, including the hair around their temples, even though this is expressly forbidden by Lev. 19:27. How should they die?*

9. *1 know from Lev. 11:6-8 that touching the skin of a dead pig makes me unclean, but may I still play football if I wear gloves?*

10. *My uncle has a farm. He violates Lev.19:19 by planting two different crops in the same field, as does his wife by wearing garments made of two different kinds of thread (cotton/polyester blend). He also tends to curse and blaspheme a lot. Is it really necessary that we go to all the trouble of getting the whole town together to stone them (Lev.24:10-16)? Couldn't we just burn them to*

*death at a private family affair, like we do with people
who sleep with their in-laws? (Lev. 20:14)*

*I know you have studied these things extensively and thus enjoy
considerable expertise in such matters, so I am confident you can help.*

The points I wish to make concern the way we prioritize Scripture,
that is, the way we use or neglect, underline or ignore biblical
passages. The original e-mail was prompted by a statement of
the purported addressee regarding marriage, and the authority
upon which that stance was based – in this case, God, and, by
implication, the Bible. Western culture has had a long tradition of
understanding marriage as a contract between one man and one
woman. The same understanding seems basic in the cultures in
which the Bible was written. The clearest supporting passage is one
in which Jesus (Mark 10:5-9), citing the book of Genesis (2:24),
declares that "a man shall leave his father and mother and be joined
to his wife." But the tradition is not without exceptions, and so
other readers of the Bible see other texts and raise other questions.

For one thing, passages abound, especially in the Hebrew
Scriptures, in which women are regarded as property, thus
the e-mail reference to selling a daughter. There are also a
considerable number of passages — the stories of Jacob, David,
and Solomon prominent among them — in which polygamy and
concubinage, while not the norm and not generally practiced,
are accepted, illustrating that in the Bible we find a variety of
what we might term "marital options." Polygamy was also known
and accepted in some early Christian communities, as it is in
Christian communities in some parts of the world today; thus the
restriction that a bishop (or "overseer") should be the husband of
one wife[13] (I Timothy 3:2) – a pointless restriction if there were
no Christians with more than one wife.

---

13 Reading with the footnote in NRSV, a more accurate reading and
   less ambiguous than the "married only once" of the main text,
   which could be read to exclude, e.g., a man who had remarried
   after being widowed.

In the e-mail, the first point raises the issue of slavery, nowhere condemned in the Jewish or Christian Bible. The third points out that in many areas of modern life, biblical categories of "clean" and "unclean" no longer seem relevant. Throughout the e-mail, though never explicitly stated, is a question about our understanding of the biblical term "abomination." (It should be pointed out that at least three different Hebrew words were translated "abomination" in the King James Version of the Bible. Some modern translations, including the New Revised Standard Version, attempt to distinguish the words through the use of synonyms such as "abhorrent", "detestable", etc.)

A very pertinent issue in this whole matter of "non-heterosexuality" (a more accurate term than "homosexuality") is the issue of finding ways to illustrate what I believe to be most certainly true: that the problem for the church is not really a theological issue, nor an issue of accepting or rejecting what the Bible says, but is really an issue of simple prejudice. I realize that the term sounds harsh. I can only say that I was raised with the same prejudice, held it without question for a majority of my life, and was able to get past it only slowly, reluctantly, and with the help of study, prayer, and friends both straight and gay. In what I present next, I have borrowed from a number of people, although I believe none of this argument is copyrighted.

Let us start with a question: What is generally accepted by Christians and Jews as the summary of the divine law? Most would cite the Ten Commandments. In the Ten Commandments, only one sexual sin is named: the sin of adultery. The term "adultery" has a specific meaning. It does not refer to just any sexual liaison apart from marriage, but to a man having sexual intercourse with a married woman not his wife (as in Leviticus 20:10 and Deuteronomy 22:22. Note that the commandment is presented from a male point of view). To be sure, the legal codes of the Old Testament also prescribe penalties for rape, incest, and male-to-male same-sex intercourse, but we might say that none of those offenses "made it into the top ten." The penalties for sexual offenses are severe: being "cut off from their people," death, death by stoning, or death by burning. Adultery is one such offense; both the man and the woman are to be put to death. There are exceptions in cases concerning the rape of an engaged woman, an unmarried woman who is not engaged, or a woman who is a slave (Leviticus 19, Deuteronomy 22).

Here is the point: adultery is named in the Ten Commandments. In both Leviticus and Deuteronomy, prohibitions against adultery appear in the same chapters as the prohibition against male-to-male intercourse, and in each case earlier in the chapter; which would seem to require that adultery be dealt with at least as severely as same-sex sexual contact. But, though it would be saying far too much to say adultery is accepted in our society, it would be accurate to say it is tolerated in society and in most churches as a lamentable "weakness of the flesh." Persons who are known to have committed adultery and many who have confessed to adultery serve in a variety of active roles in the church, including the ministry, and serve in public life, including seeking high political office. Society and church have chosen to soften the biblical judgments and penalties.

Prejudice is also exposed by our selective application of the biblical term "abomination." That is probably the main point of the supposed e-mail. In one sense that is unavoidable; every interpreter of the Bible, and one could say every reader, prioritizes texts and teachings. The Bible contains so much material, written at different times and in different circumstances, that the old claim "one can prove anything from the Bible" has some validity. But prioritizing is not the same as cherry-picking. Serious students of Scripture develop a basis for prioritizing (the technical word is a "hermeneutic") to guide their interpretation. The inconsistent use of Scripture critiqued in the e-mail and shared by many Christians – including many who, as preachers and teachers, have a more solemn responsibility in regard to the Bible – is a prime example of cherry-picking and, as such, deserves to be challenged.

Merriam-Webster's Collegiate Dictionary defines "abominable" as "worthy of or causing disgust or hatred." Though I have no supporting evidence, it is my impression that when Christians think of the word in its biblical context, it is generally understood to express God's own very strongly negative judgment. I have encountered more than a few church members who, not themselves condemning gay or lesbian friends, feel obliged (at least in the presence of a pastor) to express condemnatory views of homosexuality, believing God and Scripture require such views. One speaker at a recent (2007) conference quoted the lament of Jonathan Swift, "How is it that we have enough religion to hate one another but not enough to love one another"?

But returning to the word, "abomination", we find it used of much more than homosexuality, much more than a laundry list of sexual offenses. As mentioned in a previous chapter, we learn in the story of Joseph (Genesis 43:32) that Egyptians regarded it as an abomination (we might say, "disgusting") to eat with Hebrews. As we see in the circulated e-mail printed at the beginning of this chapter, the same law-code that declares male-to-male sex to be an abomination also uses the term to forbid planting two kinds of crops in a field or wearing clothing made of two kinds of fabric. The point is that if one uses the biblical term "abomination" as grounds for condemnation of homosexuality, one must then be willing to explain the basis on which some "abominations" remain abominable and others do not. If some see acceptance of non-heterosexuals as avoiding the clear word of Scripture, others might point out that farming with mules, planting pumpkins in cornfields, or wearing blended fabrics are also contrary to the clear word (Leviticus 19:19).

Some may explain away such inconsistency on the basis that God's mind has changed, but most would hesitate to make such an assertion. More likely, even Christians who claim to read the Bible literally actually make individual or group judgments as to which parts of the Bible still apply and which do not. But the deeper question is whether we understand and take seriously the fact that cultural factors were present in the writing of the text and are an inescapable part of our task of interpretation. Elsewhere in this book you will find mention of two scholars, Dr. Ed. Miller of the University of Colorado and Dr. Robert A. J. Gagnon of Pittsburgh Theological Seminary, who have written on the topic of homosexuality and the Bible. Both contribute valuable word studies and quite careful and extensive analyses of texts. But both seem to assume that the texts with which they work are statements of eternally valid moral principles. Neither gives adequate attention to the most basic questions: What is the Bible? To what degree might these texts be expressions of cultural norms of the societies from which they proceed?

It is certain that some will continue to struggle with the issue of non-heterosexual orientation and conduct on the grounds that it strikes them as "worthy of or causing disgust or hatred." But without getting too clinical, let me point out that the entire spectrum of sex acts: oral, anal, promiscuous, sado-masochistic, etc., is also known to be practiced by heterosexuals. Since long before Kinsey's studies, people have been aware that what some find erotic, others find shocking and disgusting – that is, *abominable.*

Perhaps you have noted, as well, that the ground on which non-heterosexuality is judged to be offensive keeps shifting – another clue that we are dealing not with reasoned argument, but with prejudice. Until perhaps a generation ago, the prejudice was defended by supposedly learned analysis; it was a "mental disorder." Among the general populace homosexuals were referred to with outrage or with nudges and sneers accompanied by the type of pejorative language which majorities always seem to use to diminish or dehumanize minorities. In that generation, gays and lesbians were shunned as weird, and feared as being intent on subverting the normal heterosexuality of children and youth. At other times and in other circles, and until today, the predominant charge against non-heterosexuals was the charge of promiscuity, sometimes accompanied by the litany of disgusting homosexual acts. The point was that (in contrast to "those people") *heterosexuals* are in search of, or living in, loving, faithful, committed, life-long unions.

Now the ground has shifted again. As non-heterosexuals have come out of the closet, we have discovered them to be our relatives, friends, neighbors, co-workers, fellow church members, and admired athletes and entertainers. Most of them lead quiet and peaceable lives, pose no threat to our children, and are not erotically attracted to us (surprising in view of how lovely and desirable we know ourselves to be!). They are not promiscuous, and – surprise! – they desire to establish loving, faithful, committed, life-long unions. I hope you will not consider it bad form if I remind you at this point that more than half of all marriages end in divorce, or if I call your attention to the content of the tabloid journalism found in any supermarket, or if I simply write the words *Wilt Chamberlain, Anna Nicole Smith, Travis Henry*[14]

Today other arguments are advanced to support rejection of homosexual unions, such as the argument that all children should have the benefit of having both a father and a mother – an excellent argument for those who would, then, advocate for laws to outlaw divorce and require marriage-plus-cohabitation of all heterosexuals. In our part of the real world, classrooms abound in which more than half of the students are from single-parent homes, others in which substantial percentages of the students are from "blended families." Some would-be political and religious leaders have suggested that marriage implies the willingness and ability of the partners to conceive, bear, and rear children; and (in

---

14 Wilt Chamberlain was an NBA basketball star who, in his auto-biography, claimed to have had sex with 20,000 women. Anna Nicole Smith married an aged billionaire; when she died in 2007, four men came forward claiming paternity of the young child she left behind. Travis Henry was a professional football player who, in 2007, was ordered to pay child support to 9 women for 9 children, all fathered out of wedlock.

case you failed to notice) gay or lesbian pairs lack the capability, ergo no marriage!

But I have officiated at weddings of couples past the age of child-bearing as well as young couples who knew that they would never be able to be parents. To these unions I have heard no objection, which leads me to doubt that the ability to bear children is really the issue. And raises an uncomfortable question: do many hold the conviction that heterosexuals are innately superior to non-heterosexuals? In other words, might the issue be more a matter of prejudice than we would be willing to admit? I invite you to think on these things.

Let's try an analogy. Much of the world operates with the metric system of weights and measures, in which progression from unit to unit is as simple as adding one more zero: 1, 10, 100, 1000, etc. But some parts of the world, including the United States, use a combination of a decimal system (as we do in the USA in handling money) and the British system of, e.g., inch, foot, yard, rod, mile, etc.; or teaspoon, tablespoon, cup, pint, quart, etc. With the advent of the computer age, some students learned to use binary language – sequences of 1's and 0's – to write computer language; and the "new math" taught students to manipulate varieties of numerical models – "base 5" or "base 12" as well as the comfortable "base 10" of the decimal system.

To pursue the analogy: In the area of human sexuality, we have lived for millennia with the comfortable illusion of a binary world, in which there are only 1's and 0's – women and men, male and female, all heterosexual. Now we face the fact that it has never been that simple. The Bible refers to behaviors we would think of as homosexual, reminding us that such behaviors have always existed in human societies; which moves us to begin by acknowledging a "base 4" world in which we find heterosexual and lesbian women, heterosexual and gay men. But there is more: we are challenged as well to reckon with the phenomenon of bisexuality, and to see it as something more than "anything goes" eroticism. And today we encounter the entire LGBTQ community: lesbian, gay, bisexual, transgendered, queer; a "community" only in the sense of being regularly confronted with the same prejudices. And, to move beyond even that, we learn of intersex children, born with genital configurations that challenge doctors and parents to make judgments and decisions regarding the sexual identity of the child, and we learn of genetic anomalies that pose challenges to surgeons, geneticists, and psychiatrists. The world of sexuality, as the world of mathematics, is not as simple and straight-forward as we had once innocently assumed.

All of which raises two challenges. One, to be addressed in more detail in another chapter, is the challenge of having "enough religion to love one another." A problem in this regard is that so much public discussion seems focused on hypothetical people. Real people have a way of getting to your heart. And you stop thinking of them as caricatures or in terms of categories. I was reminded of this in a conversation with the church office administrator. Sexual orientation was under discussion. She had lesbians and gays as friends. "But how about in your family?" I asked. "Yes, a brother-in-law." Then it was my turn. "I don't . . . wait, yes I do! My cousin, Tim, is gay. I've known it for a few years, but I'd forgotten. He's just Tim." And Tim has a partner, and another friend named Ben is gay, and Maya prefers the term "queer." But since I've gotten to know them, all of that seems less and less relevant. They are people, most of them church members, who work and pray and shop and travel and give and sing or teach or serve coffee. They worry, and get sick, and laugh, and pay mortgage or rent, and love their families, and have hobbies, and relax with friends, and may live in a committed relationship. And yearn for acceptance and justice. And sexual attraction has about the same place in their lives as in yours. It is not the one factor that defines them.

Jason was thrown off balance. More than a decade earlier he and Christine and Joel had met at a young adults group at their church and had become best friends. Jason and Christine eventually married, Joel remaining a special friend. A few years later, when Steven was born, Joel was asked to be one of his baptismal sponsors. Joel's work had taken him to another state, but he returned often, and never failed to spend some time with Jason and Christine. And, as a faithful sponsor, he remained close to Steve. But now (I know you're ahead of me on this) Joel had come out of the closet, told Jason and Christine that he was gay. And Jason was stunned. "I've always had this opinion about homosexuals," he told me. "I have thought of them as bad, people you wouldn't want around your children. But I know Joel as a friend and as a Christian. I would never have a qualm about him spending time with Steve, whether it was going camping or whatever. I trust him completely. And I realize that I have some rethinking to do."

Being gay was a reality in Joel's life, but not a factor that got in the way of his other relationships, or of his faith, or his care for the Christian nurture of a child to whom he had been bound by water and Spirit. The bonds of faith and friendship between Jason, Christine, and Joel are as strong as ever.

One challenge, as I said, is the challenge of having enough faith to love one another. The second challenge is thinking through the fears, concerns, and prejudices that see acceptance of sexual variations as a threat to an ordered society. Although my primary concerns are theologically- and justice-oriented, and I do not see the ordering of society as an area in which I have special expertise, I will attempt to make some relevant observations.

It is well-established in law that the state has an interest in defining and regulating marriage. Courts have also been obliged to make judgments with regard to a number of "marriage equivalents", historically including common-law marriage and more recently couples without legally recognized relationships; that is, cohabiting couples, including those who are gay and lesbian. Relationships without legal sanction have existed at many times and places. To take one example: though polygamy is not legally accepted in any of the 50 U.S. states, it is no longer criminalized, and is known to exist in a number of states, especially among fundamentalist Latter-Day Saints (Mormon) sects. In cases where there have been allegations that individuals in these polygamist sects have committed rape or incest, or have caused other harm to the welfare of minor girls, the states have intervened and brought suit against the individuals involved in these alleged crimes. Where such criminal conduct is not at issue, the states have usually refrained from prosecution on the basis of the difficulty in bringing successful prosecution and are restrained from prosecution by the "consenting adults" principle. But the exceptions have not abolished the rule.

But in some other circumstances, restraints on marriage have been altered or removed. Limits on the degree of blood relationship permitted in marriage have been amended in a variety of ways by the various states. Prohibitions of inter-racial marriage, once common in the U.S., have been removed. Though a Colorado cowboy, many years ago, obtained a marriage license to marry his horse, that is universally recognized as a humorous aberration and not as the opening of a door to rampant inter-species sexuality.

My point is that it is difficult to see how granting the right to any two consenting adults to form a legally-recognized relationship including a wide array of legally-recognized rights would in any way threaten the fabric of society. And to apply the recognized terminology of "marriage" would clarify the relationship in the eyes of community and society without in any way impinging on the relationships or the rights of other couples, gay or straight. To be sure, "gray-area" or illicit relationships would continue to exist – think of the example of polygamy cited above, or think of "open marriages", communes, or the like. Despite the existence of such forms of living arrangements and sexual activity, we live in a relatively ordered society, in which community standards establish the rough parameters. There is no reason to think that the recognition of loving, faithful, committed relationships between homosexual partners would change that.

Chapter 5
Life Outside of Eden

It is said that as a man stood talking with his friend, a neighbor approached and asked if he might borrow a rope. "I'm sorry," the man replied, "but I plan to be using the rope to tie up some sand." When the neighbor had departed, the friend said, "Your reply made no sense. How can you use a rope to tie up sand?" And the man replied, "If you don't want to let someone have something, any reason will do."

Let us think of life in the church in this way: *It is life with God, in community, outside of Eden, for the sake of the world.*

In thinking about Scripture and sexuality we have been looking at Scripture from an angle not customarily taken in sermons or Bible studies, and have been looking at sexuality from a straight-forward, "real world" perspective. We live in world of relationships – relationships at times wonderful, at times difficult, at times muddled. How we relate to others, whether or to what degree we are willing to understand and accept one another, is a basic issue in the church's struggle with non-heterosexuality.

I have heard and read the comments of many people who are troubled by the church's exploration of these issues. The concerns have been phrased in a variety of ways, but all have focused on what people who are not heterosexual should be or do. The simplest solution suggested is that they should simply be heterosexual. The next suggestion is that they should abandon any desire for relationships that are other than platonic; in other words, no intimate, physical, sexual contact. But the third concern is the one we address now; the suggestion that what is lacking on the part of "those people" is sufficient confession, sufficient repentance, sufficient concern for righteousness. Could they not, at the least, give evidence of more shame, and more self-reproach, and practice *celibacy*?

But I would prefer to turn the conversation in a different direction. For me, the question is not "Who are they?" but "Who are we, all of us together?" A related question is, "What does it mean to be church?" or "How do we understand life in the church?" The answer I propose is that it is *life with God, in community, outside of Eden, for the sake of the world.*

Life with God is a gift; life in community is a gift; life outside of Eden is a challenge; life for the sake of the world, for the sake of our neighbor, is our mission. Because we are "outside of Eden," living in a fallen world, our relationship with God includes not only prayer, praise and thanksgiving, but also daily confession and repentance, daily forgiveness, and daily prayers for renewal and righteousness. All of which is true for heterosexuals and non-heterosexuals alike. It is to these topics we now turn.

Confession and Repentance

Confession is admission of our wrongs. In traditional liturgical language, it is the admission that we have sinned "in thought, word, and deed." Repentance is a change in attitude or action, a change of direction, having our heart and mind renewed. By way of illustration, consider the functioning of human society. When a person is guilty of antisocial acts, behaviors that harm or threaten the neighbor, society assigns punishments in an effort to protect the neighbor and society and to bring about a change of attitude or behavior. For traffic offenses, fines are levied and, on occasion, jail time. For stalkers, restraining orders are issued; for road rage, anger management, etc. We learned in kindergarten (figure of speech: there were no kindergartens in rural South Dakota when I was a child) to apologize for harming, offending or mistreating another person, and we still do it.

Before God we confess those things which trouble us, or which lead us to recognize our brokenness, our faults and failings, whether in thought, word, or deed. And we join the Psalmist in lamenting, *"...the ordinances of the LORD are true and righteous altogether. ... Moreover by them is your servant warned; in keeping them there is great reward. But who can detect their errors? Clear me from hidden faults."* (Psalm 19:12)

We all carry within us our own perceptions concerning our own faults, we repent as faith and heart lead us, and we often assign our own penance. But it is also lamentably true that we too easily occupy ourselves with our perceptions concerning the faults of others. Lacking power to assign penance in any formal way, we would still like to preempt the place of God by making *our* determination concerning how *others* ought to repent. Some become too easily preoccupied with the thought that persons who are not heterosexual should focus their repentance on sexual abstinence and amendment of the sexual side of life.

For that matter, we cannot know how much *heterosexual* repentance is focused on the sexual dimension of life. But we do know the things commonly included in confessional statements, both liturgical and personal: we confess that we have not loved God whole-heartedly and have not loved our neighbors as ourselves, we lament self-centeredness, bad temper, conflicts with coworkers, tendencies toward greed, thoughtless words spoken, anxiety despite the promises of God, neglect of worship and prayer, too little time spent with family and friends, etc. And I think it quite possible that items listed by non-heterosexuals are very like the "lament and confession" lists of heterosexuals. It would not surprise me to learn that desires for love and intimacy are not often part of the list; and that non-heterosexuals also include the words of the Psalmist concerning "hidden faults" as a way of asking God's forgiveness for things seen as faults from heaven's perspective but not recognized as such in one's own eyes.

To which I would add one point: is it possible that the tendency to reject those who are not heterosexual and to attempt to restrict their lives should have larger place in the confession and repentance of the heterosexual majority? Might attitudes of rejection, grudging acceptance, or "welcoming, but not affirming" be ways in which the church does wrong to our neighbors? Seeing the mote in the eyes of the other, do we overlook the log in our own? In a video produced by the Rocky Mountain Synod of the ELCA, one of the presenters stated that in therapy, 28% of persons identified as homosexuals make some degree of progress in moving away from that orientation or, at least, in their ability to function in a more heterosexual way. I do not know the source of the statistic, but I know that some sources give a lower percentage. Based on the fact that members of this target group have entered therapy with change of orientation or function as their goal, I would assume that they are quite highly motivated, and not a cross-section of the non-heterosexual population. Yet, the statistic informs us that even so motivated, 72% *did not make progress* toward the stated goal.

I certainly have no issue with individuals entering therapy to explore personal issues, including issues of sexuality, sexual orientation, or gender identity. Therapy can be extremely helpful for working through issues of sexuality as through other issues. And I can readily understand therapy as an option chosen by one who is already married and trying to come to terms with a recently-recognized orientation out of a desire to maintain marriage and family life with loved ones; or by a young person observing or experiencing the rejection homosexuals face in society and hoping to avoid that pain and price; or by one with a literal understanding of Scripture hoping to avoid the condemnation of God and church. For such persons or for others therapy may be an appropriate option. But I lament the pressures, internal and external, that often persuade non-heterosexuals that therapy, with change of orientation as the goal, should be undertaken because their orientation is somehow seen as wrong. It should go without saying that when therapy is chosen it should be with a competent therapist and not with one whose agenda is to change the client's orientation. The statistic cited above shows that 72% of non-heterosexuals, even though highly motivated, did not experience any significant change, which conveys a clear message that orientation is not as changeable (or "mutable") as some insist it is. It is something other than a "chosen" "lifestyle".

Righteousness, Law, and St. Paul's Summary

We might also address the occasionally heard concern that homosexuals should give greater attention to "righteousness". As I understand it, this concern is usually based on two specific criticisms of homosexual behavior. One is the global HIV/AIDS epidemic. Though AIDS in Africa is today a predominantly heterosexual epidemic, and heterosexual AIDS cases are multiplying around the world, it first appeared as a disease afflicting primarily homosexual males and intravenous drug users. In the early years, some preachers spoke of it as "God's judgment on gays". The stigma remains in many minds: AIDS, promiscuity, and homosexuality go together. The second criticism of homosexual behavior arises from memories of some first generation "Gay Pride" parades which featured blatant and promiscuous homosexuality.

But while those criticisms and images may be in our minds, they are not the current issues before the church. There is, in fact, a certain irony in the fact that while homosexuals have traditionally been assailed for being promiscuous, they are now being assailed for desiring lifelong, committed unions. And, in fact, a great many non-heterosexuals are no more promiscuous than a great many heterosexuals, which may or may not offer comfort to those of us who have concerns regarding our sexuality-charged culture.

But when we speak of righteousness, we should also do so theologically. Lutheran theology and the Confessions speak of righteousness in two senses. One is "civil righteousness" which is not "saving righteousness," but is a matter of acting, choosing, and restraining oneself in a variety of ways for the sake of the neighbor and for the sake of good order in society. This is a righteousness based on the law, and helps us live in society. The second type of righteousness is "saving righteousness" often referred to as "imputed" – the righteousness before God which we receive as a gift for the sake of Jesus Christ, and which frees us to be God's people in society.

Civil righteousness based on law undergoes a degree of development and transformation within the Bible. Parts of the Torah consist of law codes that are detailed and specific, the "Holiness Code" of Leviticus perhaps preeminent among them. In the Prophets and the Psalms concern for this type of righteousness is stated with a different emphasis in various summary formulae stressing relationship to God; emphasizing justice, love, kindness, and mutual respect; and often presented in forms less related to detailed individual behaviors and religious rituals than are the law codes of the Torah. Psalm 51 and other penitential Psalms could serve as examples, as could familiar passages from Isaiah, Amos, Micah and other prophets

In the New Testament, St. Paul's passion to see Gentiles enfolded in the church led him to earnest wrestling with the law, especially in terms of the relationship between law and grace, law and promise. The Pauline and deutero-Pauline letters speak of the "accusing law", accompanied by a call to trust in Christ alone, in line with the conviction (later restated by Luther and others) that we are justified by grace alone through faith alone. Though Paul was strongly opposed to license or "lawlessness" (recognizing the dangers of unrestrained human nature), he understood Christian obedience to be based on something other than the stringent and literalistic use of the Jewish law as he had known and experienced it in his earlier life. The letter to the Ephesians (probably not from St. Paul) declares that Christ "has abolished the law with its commandments and ordinances". The foundation of Christian morality and ethics can then be understood in terms of relationships; that is, as the appropriate expression and offering of love and devotion toward God and love toward the neighbor.

The Philippian congregation is urged to "live your life in a manner worthy of the gospel of Christ." Clearer statements of the relationship between that life of "worthiness" and the "law" are found in two other places in Paul's writings, stated in summary form with virtually identical phrasing in Romans 13 and Galatians 5: "Love does no wrong to a neighbor; therefore, love is the fulfilling of the law". In those passages we see Paul's "law", his concept of obedience. We should be clear, of course, that in those and related passages Paul is not writing of what the Confessions term "imputed (saving) righteousness", but of "civil righteousness". As I read Paul's arguments, I understand it to be his position that the standard against which civil righteousness is to be measured is not by its adherence to the law codes of the Torah, but by its effect on the life of the neighbor. So, let us take another look at life in community.

Life in Community

We simply do not know what St. Paul would have said had he possessed the same information and been confronted by the same quandaries we face today. He most certainly would have continued to maintain that all of us, including homosexuals, have no hope except the grace of God which is ours in Christ Jesus. And if his references in the vice lists were to temple prostitution (if such a practice actually existed; vigorous debate continues), pederasty, and other blatant and promiscuous sexual activity, he would certainly see such practices as no less appalling. But what would he have said of Christians desiring to live in committed relationships? I would suggest that none of us can answer with complete certainty. For me, the answer must come not from the passages listed, but from the gospel.

I would concede that the sciences are uncertain as to the causative factors in homosexuality and other varieties of sexual orientation and identity. Are these chosen behaviors, or factors rooted in our genetic code? Do they result from things done or neglected by our parents? Do experiences in early childhood play a part? Speaking personally, *I do not know*, though I tend to give more credibility to those who are themselves non-heterosexual and to the scientists who simply accept the phenomenon as a given rather than as a disorder. More importantly, in terms of my thought process and pastoral approach, the question of causation is irrelevant. What is known is that most homosexuals insist that they have not chosen their orientation. They ask why they would have chosen to be misunderstood, excluded, and ostracized. Some report early memories of same-sex attraction, others made sincere efforts to live as heterosexuals and finally conceded defeat in those efforts. They are convinced that their orientation was not a simple matter of choice. And the vast majority of psychologists and counselors report that, even with extensive therapy, very few can be reoriented to live happily as heterosexuals.

But I do know that Scripture, even as it contains that short list of passages often quoted against non-heterosexuals, is also filled with cautions against judging others, and with admonitions for Christians to love one another, *"for love covers a multitude of sins."* (I Peter 4:8) I know some think that homosexuals, however they may have come to their orientation, are condemned to live apart from precious experiences of human life and relationship.

Let me say that everything I know of the gospel argues against that. Rather, I am persuaded that "there is no distinction"; that God's grace, which is sufficient to enfold heterosexuals as full participants in the life of the church, is also sufficient to include LGBTQ persons within the same community of faith and hope and love. And if so, ought we not simply apply to them the same "vision and expectations" rubrics which apply to heterosexuals?

I have emphasized my concern that we exercise some degree of consistency and evenhandedness in our use of Scripture. On what basis do we read St. Paul's argument that "all have sinned and fall short of the glory of God," and yet seek to identify "homosexuals" as a special category of sinners beyond the rest? On what biblical or rational basis can we argue for elevating "homosexuality" to be a category of sin worse than greed and materialism, which are clearly more frequently condemned in the Bible? Is it possible that we might, at least in some cases, approach texts or the whole topic with a wish to "trust in ourselves that we are righteous and regard others with contempt?" (a paraphrase of Luke 18:9)

A number of the parables of Jesus are directed against prejudice and judgment. Prominent among them are the parable of the Good Samaritan (Luke 10:25-37), the parable of the Weeds in the Wheat (Matthew 13:24-30), and the parable of the Dragnet (Matthew 13:47-50). The New Testament also contains warnings against judging, as in Romans 2:1, *"...in passing judgment on another you condemn yourself ...,"* Matthew 7:1, *"Do not judge, so that you may not be judged,"* and the parallel in Luke 6:37. It is true that Christians are advised to teach and admonish one another (Colossians 3:16b), but also to bear one another's burdens (Galatians 6:2), and to remember that judgment belongs to the Lord.

Certainly the existence of non-heterosexuals in society does not alter my heterosexuality, nor threaten my marriage, nor lead to fears of the extinction of the human race. Jesus said nothing about it, and the New Testament makes much stronger statements in opposition to wealth and greed. It poses no greater threat of violence or harm to individuals or society than does heterosexuality. And, as this book attempts to point out, the argument against it from Scripture is not as clear and rock-solid as some would suppose. It is time for the church to get over its phobia about sexual orientation, and instead to give attention to, and guidance on, issues related to behaviors. Such attention and guidance could be equally addressed to, and be equally pertinent for, both heterosexuals and homosexuals. The draft study on Human Sexuality released by the ELCA in 2008 is a very cautious, positive beginning in this regard, though it studiously avoids implying that non-heterosexuals should be regarded and treated as fully equal to heterosexuals in the life of the church and on the rosters of the denomination.

It is, unfortunately, all too common to find Christians making gratuitous prejudicial statements against homosexuals; statements which would not be tolerated if made regarding other minorities. Some make the blanket assumption that all homosexuals have "chosen" a "lifestyle" and that all are promiscuous. Learned individuals have made comments in church and quasi-church publications, and in other materials distributed to congregations, reflecting an assumption that gays and lesbians wish to seduce children and youth and somehow turn them into homosexuals.

As a pastor with extensive parish ministry experience, I have encountered a substantial number of gay and lesbian Christians. I can only say that in light of my experience, the statements to which I refer in the preceding paragraph stand as egregious violations of the 8th Commandment. I have encountered persons in long-term, faithful relationships; have seen fondness and care continue between two Christians even after their 20-year marriage was ended by the sexual orientation of one of the partners; have known non-heterosexuals who were among the most faithful, prayerful, Word-centered, committed, caring and sensitive Christians I have encountered. These are our sisters and brothers, our nieces, nephews, and grandchildren, having no less need for acceptance, love and intimacy; having no less capacity for love, commitment, and faithfulness than the rest of us.

I do not doubt that some have encountered the "seamy side" of homosexuality, and have found it to be degraded, disgusting, horrifying, *(please insert additional adjectives here)*. But as a pastor I have also encountered some who have lived the seamy side of heterosexuality, and have learned more than I have encountered. It is also degraded, disgusting, horrifying *(please insert duplicate list of adjectives here)*. It is unworthy of Christians to define one group – in this case, heterosexuals – on the basis of the best that group has to offer and to define another group – in this case, homosexuals – on the basis of the worst examples to be found within it.

In recent years, some segments of society, including a number of political leaders and members of various legislative bodies, have been declaring their anxiety over (and opposition to) "gay marriage". No one has yet explained to me what harm a "gay marriage" would do to the more-than-50-year marriage in which my wife and I live with joy. We have not suffered from the fact that other *heterosexual* pairs live in relationships having the same title as ours, and fail to understand how we would be harmed by *homosexual* couples united in marriage. It seems fully appropriate to us that people who wish to live together in love and faithfulness within a committed union, whatever their orientation, should be able to share living space; tax status and insurance benefits; have visitation rights in times of illness and survivor benefits at the time of death; beget, adopt, and rear children as biology and law permit; etc., etc., just as we do. To us, all of that sounds pretty much like marriage.

Let me say three things before closing this section. First, I have doubts about the theological integrity of a position which declares that homosexuals should be entitled to "full participation in all aspects of parish life" on one hand, and restricts them from ordained status on the other hand. The policy exists in the absence of a rationale. It may be true that homosexuals are statistically more likely to be promiscuous or commit anti-social acts than heterosexuals (*may be* true – what I observe and read of heterosexual conduct makes me dubious). But if we were to follow that logic, we would ordain only women. We would not ordain males because statistics are not in their favor.

Second, on the basis of creation theology, it seems unworthy of us to expect "celibacy in singleness" of persons who are denied any possibility of non-single status in relationships. Can we not simply ask faithfulness in committed relationships (and why not "marriage"?) of all rostered leaders of our church? To demand celibacy is itself an injustice in view of the church's refusal to recognize or provide an avenue to approved faithful relationships. As pointed out in a previous chapter, the current policy of the ELCA contradicts Luther's clear statement in his Large Catechism explanation of the Sixth Commandment. Recognizing committed and blessed same-gender relationships to be marriage would clarify the status of those relationships in a way that would benefit the couples involved, as well as their friends, families, congregations, and the wider society.

And, third, it appears to me that when the church denies its blessing to committed same-sex relationships it is actually, if unintentionally, expressing a preference for casual and promiscuous behaviors. In I Corinthians, St. Paul affirms the value of the recognized, regularized relationship of marriage as a way to control and channel passion. In my understanding, he is making the point that in the absence of such recognized relationships, passions easily go out of control. I doubt that denying blessing to heterosexual couples would result in increased celibacy among heterosexuals, and I doubt that attempts to deny loving, physical relationships to non-heterosexuals is of any benefit to them or to society.

Life Outside of Eden

You know how you sometimes respect people who irritate you? The parents of one lesbian woman I know continue to do all they can to divide her from her partner. Invitations are pointedly individual, the existence of the partner scarcely acknowledged, siblings discouraged from expressing inclusion, welcome, or acceptance. I understand their struggle. The tradition in which they were raised declares only heterosexuality acceptable: any other orientation is sinful. Such attitudes irritate me. But these parents also have my utmost respect. When their daughter and her partner pledged to one another their love and faithfulness, they were there! Unhappy, to be sure, contrary to their original intention, to be sure, and not without tears, they were there. Perhaps my words made a difference. I had phoned them the day before, asked them to come. The point I tried to make was that I and many others respected their daughter and her partner, affirmed the relationship, and their presence couldn't be a mistake. Even if all else was wrong, even though they opposed the decision she had made, their presence would affirm their love for their daughter. Whether the relationship endured or (as they fervently hoped) fell apart, there was more reason to attend than to avoid.

A number of Paul's letters contain "tables of duties," advice and exhortation concerning how Christians are to live with one another in various relationships: husband and wife, parent and child, master and slave, church member and church member, Christian and government, etc. These sections remind us of a truth important for the relationships in those letters, relevant to the anecdote related above, and vitally important in the current discussions within the ELCA. That truth is that you and I live in a world far removed from Eden, with no option in human society or in the church but to keep trying to learn how to live with one another outside of Eden.

The challenge for humanity, and especially for humans who seek to know and serve God, is to discriminate between those things that are truly evil, destructive of community and the welfare of the neighbor; and those things which we may see as harming community because they offend our opinions or sensibilities, but in actuality do no harm to the neighbor. In the latter case, the one who is offended (or chooses to be) may be the one actually harming both the community and the rejected neighbor.

Human history has featured one solution to the problem of life outside Eden: separation, exclusion, rejection, hostility, and – ultimately – destruction of the "other". This solution is, in the truest sense, a "process of elimination". In the '60s Bernard Backman[15] produced a reading set to music titled, "Reverse Creation". The reading depicts humanity day by day destroying the goodness of the creation. On the day before the end, they write, "And finally man said, 'Let us create God in our own image,... let us say God thinks as we think, and hates as we hate, and kills as we kill.'" It has been so. From ancient tribal rivalries, to the Crusades, to the great wars (both "hot" and "Cold") of the 20th Century, to segregation and apartheid, to the ongoing reciprocal destruction resulting from terrorism and the "War on Terror", humanity has pursued this solution with zeal.

Yet the New Testament insists this is not God's will or God's "vision" for the creation. God's desire is *"to reconcile to himself all things, whether on earth or in heaven, by making peace through the blood of (Christ's) cross"* (Ephesians 1:20). The Pentecost story of Acts 2 reunites what was divided in the story of the Tower of Babel. Communication is restored and scattered humanity "from every nation under heaven" gathered in a brief foretaste of heaven. Because that which has been truly accomplished in Christ has not come to its ultimate completion, causes of offense and temptations to separation continue to plague the world and the church. But in this confusing world, Christians are charged to *"maintain constant love for one another, for love covers a multitude of sins"* (I Peter 4:8). And I Corinthians 13:13 declares that *"faith, hope, and love abide, these three; and the greatest of these is love."*

---

15 Backman, Bernard A. from original album <u>Portrait of Man</u>, 1969.

It is my hope that the road will not be long – the road we walk as we talk together and come to decisions within our churches regarding these sisters and brothers who endure such scrutiny. As I stated in the Introduction, I believe the issues cannot be settled simply by quoting Scripture. But I believe there is room in Scripture, and certainly in our understanding of the gospel, for us to move to new levels of understanding and action in relationship to our gay, lesbian, bisexual, and transgendered sisters and brothers. It is my hope that my denomination, the ELCA, will soon come to gospel-compelled decisions in favor of full acceptance.

For life outside Eden, no doubt living together in "love that does no wrong to a neighbor" will be the best we can do. A commitment from members of the Body of Christ to make that our aim would certainly be a marvelous beginning.

Chapter 6
Welcome is Our Mission

The title of this chapter raises an immediate question. How can *welcome* be said to be our mission? The mission of the church is to proclaim Christ crucified. The mission is to tell the good news of Christ's resurrection. The mission is to spread the gospel. The mission is to proclaim the forgiveness of sins. But *welcome?* The question is appropriate. One could imagine varieties of welcome taking place apart from the proclamation of Christ, apart from the declaration of sin forgiven, apart from any specific witness to Christ and the church. Many people are hospitable without faith in or reference to God. Certainly, welcome is not a stand-alone expression of our mission.

But I would argue that no other statement of the church's mission is adequate or authentic apart from welcome. Welcome can undoubtedly exist apart from the mission. But the mission cannot take place apart from welcome, or, if you prefer, hospitality. But "welcome" is a familiar word in the Bible. The case could be argued in great detail, but brief comments will serve to illustrate. In Jesus' familiar parable of the Last Judgment, the first charge leveled by the king against those on the left hand is, *"I was a stranger, and you did not welcome me."* (Matthew 25:43) The gospel message proclaimed by Paul is one of reconciliation. *"In Christ God was reconciling the world to himself, not counting their trespasses against them, and entrusting the message of reconciliation to us."* (2 Corinthians 5:19) And, again, *"...we even boast in God through our Lord Jesus Christ, through whom we have now received reconciliation."* (Romans 5:11) Reconciliation is illustrated by an embrace, a handshake, some gesture of welcome. Jesus' summary of the law in the two great commandments is expressed in terms of love for God and for neighbor. And love can hardly be genuine where there is no welcome, no embrace.

Ephesians declares the will of God *"...to gather up all things in (Christ)...."* As it pertains to life in this world, the goal of the gospel is for people to live with God and one another in harmony. Again, hear St. Paul, *"May the God of steadfastness and encouragement grant you to live in harmony with one another, in accordance with Christ Jesus, so that together you may with one voice glorify the God and Father of our Lord Jesus Christ. Welcome one another, therefore, just as Christ has welcomed you, for the glory of God."* (Romans 15:5-7)

Life in Christ, life with God, life in Christian community is characterized by reaching across the divisions so prevalent in our world to welcome, include, restore. Welcome is a key element in, and a fair characterization of, the church's mission.

In his understanding of that mission, the Rev. Jim Siefkes was a pioneer. He was the staff member of The American Lutheran Church who was the moving force in the relationship of the ALC to the University of Minnesota program on human sexuality. That program, originally designed as part of the medical school curriculum, was expanded to include seminary students and church agency social workers. Because it raised concerns in church circles, and because I was serving on the National Church Council of the ALC at the time, my wife, Marlys, and I chose to participate. Our attendance was a very positive experience. We learned that the "concerns" were based on the frankness and openness with which sexuality and sexual orientation were presented and discussed. Presenters included not only heterosexual couples and singles, but also persons with disabilities and disabling medical conditions, the elderly, and, of course, gays and lesbians. It was in the context of that program that Marlys and I first had opportunity to meet and hear persons who were both openly gay and openly Christian, and to gain a greater appreciation of the vital importance of understanding and of welcome.

As the previous chapter, and the last of the "Resources" at the end of the book make clear, I support the legal recognition of committed relationships, whether the orientation of the partners be heterosexual or not.

So, when Lauri and Andrea asked if I would conduct a ceremony to bless their relationship, I was happy to do so. But this isn't about me, it is about their congregation. The congregation welcomed and embraced them, hosted their rehearsal dinner and their reception, brought gifts and flowers, attended and congratulated them. And continues to list their anniversaries. They are supported, affirmed, prayed for. The acceptance of one congregation led to acceptance by other congregations in the community. One of these women is now employed as a staff member in a congregation of another mainline and quite traditional denomination, with youth leadership a part of the job. Another serves as mentor for a confirmation student. They are blessed, and a blessing. The congregations in this story have a vision of what it means to be church: for them, it means welcome, a vital element in their mission.

As I read the Bible and live in the church, I see in each a double dynamic at work – two functions that exist in some tension with one another. We might label these dynamics "preservation" and "mission." One focuses on the identity, cohesiveness, and purity of the group. The other focuses on expanding the group, bringing others to join in accepting the faith the group confesses, and in declaring the purposes and passions of God. Both are visible in the Bible, and in both Old and New Testaments. They are discernible in God's words to Abraham, *"Go from your country and your kindred and your father's house to the land that I will show you. I will make of you a great nation (preservation), and I will bless you, and make your name great, so that you will be a blessing (mission)."* (Genesis 12:1-2) Commenting on that text, a rabbi asserted that the final part of that passage is best heard as an imperative: "Be a blessing."

Both dynamics continue in the story of the Exodus, the wilderness wandering, and the giving of the law. All were part of the "preservation" process of forming a people and binding them in relationship to God. But Israel had a mission, to be a light to the nations, a people set apart to declare God's praise. The mission dynamic continues to be visible in many places: in the story of Ruth, in Elisha healing Naaman, in the touching missionary tract of Jonah which pictures enemies turning to God as Nineveh repents (even the cattle garbed in sackcloth!), and in the prophets, notably the final section of Isaiah which pictures foreigners streaming to the temple.

But history kept intervening, and Israel was forced to devote energy to defending and defining itself over against Egyptians, Philistines, Edomites, Canaanites, Assyrians, Syrians, in a seemingly never-ending struggle. And the "preservation" function assumes the primary place; that is, the desire to affirm and define and protect the community; to develop criteria and maintain standards for inclusion and exclusion. I do not take the situation lightly. The threats were real, battles frequent. The world was and is a violent and dangerous place, inhabited by strangers and by enemies as well as by friends, fellow-countrymen, and fellow believers.

But when one's focus turns toward preservation, one perceives one's assignment in regard to the neighbor as not primarily to welcome, but to evaluate; not to embrace, but to judge. And biblical – yes, the word is "religion" – can become as rigid and exclusionary as any other, all in the name of righteousness and godliness. In a sense, our evaluation or judgment is a fruitless exercise, for Scripture declares that *"(Mortals) look on the outward*

appearance, but the LORD looks on the heart." (I Samuel 16:7c)
But, no matter, we feel an obligation and entitlement, much like
the Pharisee in the parable Jesus told, who evaluated himself over
against the tax collector standing in the corner.

But though the nations of Israel and Judah, understandably
defensive and anxious, developed inward-focused characteristics,
the most dynamic of the prophets offered a constant critique,
and sought through eloquent "re-telling" to keep declaring the
purposes and passions of God.

The New Testament has mission at its core. Yet even though
written over a period not much longer than half a century,
we still see attention given to defining and protecting the
community, especially in some of the later writings. And we see
the preservation dynamic at work in the history of the church,
especially as the church became strong and institutionalized after
the time of the Emperor Constantine. In a development that
has continued to our day, the church came to see itself as the
definer of the ethical, the defender of morality, often the patron
of the status quo; in short, as having a role similar to that of the
Pharisees as we see them in the Gospel[16]. In the Middle Ages the
church had absolute power in regard to inclusion and exclusion.
It had the power of life and death, and asserted that it had control
over heaven and hell.

But I wish to give primary attention to the New Testament
and to the mission dynamic at its core or, to say it in other words,
to give attention to the purpose of the early church. Based on a
reading of the New Testament, how did the apostles understand
their mission? I would propose that over against almost every
other religious system, the New Testament portrays a mission
marked by radical inclusion, radical hospitality. I see this dynamic
at work throughout the New Testament, but nowhere more
dramatically than in Luke-Acts and the letters of Paul.

---

16 It is widely recognized that there is some degree of caricature in
the New Testament's presentation of the Pharisees, as many New
Testament introductions and commentaries attest.

Many have commented on Luke's interest in the outcast and overlooked – Samaritans, women, the poor, lepers, tax collectors, etc. – and on the attention given to issues of wealth and poverty. The Magnificat declares that *"(God) has scattered the proud in the thoughts of their hearts. He has brought down the powerful from their thrones, and lifted up the lowly; he has filled the hungry with good things, and sent the rich away empty."* (Luke 1:51b-53) At the Nazareth synagogue, previously quoted, Jesus declares that his mission includes, "…to bring good news to the poor."

The complaint of his pious and proper critics was that *"this man receives sinners and eats with them."* (Luke 15:2) Jesus' desire to welcome the "lost" and overlooked is evident in his parables of the Lost Sheep, the Lost Coin, and the Prodigal Son; his advocacy on behalf of the excluded and despised, including the Samaritans, is seen in the story of the Ten Lepers (Luke 17:12) and the parable of the Good Samaritan (Luke 10:29-37). A universal vision is visible in Luke's genealogy of Jesus, which is traced to Adam, the father of all humanity, rather than to Abraham, the patriarch of Israel, as is the case in Matthew.

The "Great Commission" of Matthew 28 is echoed twice in Luke-Acts: in Luke 24 and Acts 1. In all three places it is specified that the mission is to "all nations." In Matthew the assignment is to "make disciples of all nations." In Luke, the disciples are told that *"repentance and forgiveness of sins is to be proclaimed in his name to all nations;"* in Acts the mission is to *"be my witnesses in Jerusalem, in all Judea and Samaria, and to the ends of the earth."* In all three, the commission represents a significant departure from the religious and ethnic attitudes the apostles had always known.

In Acts, the hammering home of this inclusive mission is unrelenting, and is paired in the early chapters with an equally unrelenting critique of the Jewish leaders, based on their rejection of Jesus; which meant rejection of his inclusive message and ministry and, pre-eminently, rejection of the apostolic witness to the resurrection.

The point that should be emphasized is that in Luke-Acts, as well as in many other places in the New Testament, those who are welcomed and included are not only those outside the law, or the ethnically "other," but those seen as morally deficient as well. Zacchaeus might serve as an example (Luke 19). Those who would be excluded according to the standards of any "proper" religious system were welcomed. In Acts, the early outreach of the new community embraced the Ethiopian eunuch (Acts 8); a converted Pharisee, Paul (Acts 9); the Roman officer, Cornelius and his family (Acts 10); and Paul's first convert – apparently a Gentile – Sergius Paulus (Acts 13). The ultimate movement of the book of Acts is as truly symbolic as it is geographic. It takes the center of the Christian community from Jerusalem to Rome, the center of a vast and diverse empire.

In an earlier chapter mention was made of the vice lists in the New Testament letters. A further brief comment on those lists seems in order. A great concern of Paul and the other early missionaries as they took the gospel to all nations was to form communities – not simply to convert individuals, but to bring them together from disparate backgrounds into the church. This meant Jews and Gentiles, to be sure, but in some parts of the Empire, and especially in seaports and trade centers, the Gentiles could be a very diverse lot.

To form a community from people of such varied backgrounds was a monumental task. The mission of the apostles involved not only proclaiming the faith, but articulating an ethic for the new community. The apostles, and especially Paul, were determined not to fall back on the restrictions of Jewish law as they had learned it, but they needed ways of talking about conduct and relationships. The vice lists provided one way of doing this – vice lists used as illustrations (as in Romans 13 and Galatians 5) of the ethic of love for neighbor. What this means is that the vice lists were not written to exclude, but were addressed to people *in* the community to make them aware of, and caution them against, neighbor-harming and community-breaking behaviors. The purpose of the lists is to serve the life of the community, which is why most of the items on those lists address such things as gossip and dissension. The "sexuality" items on those lists should be seen in that light, which cautions us against reading them in such a way as to condemn loving and faithful same-sex relationships which do no harm to neighbor or community.

The struggle of churches today as they face issues of non-heterosexuality is primarily a struggle between the "preservation" and "mission" dynamics, between what is perceived as "defending morality" and extending welcome. I am convinced that when the church sees the issue as it is, permits the whole of Scripture to speak, accepts the teaching of the sciences, and opens its eyes to see non-heterosexuals as true sisters and brothers, it will fully claim its identity and heritage and become fully welcoming.

But now that we have come this far in detailing perspectives on Scripture and sexuality, the final questions concern what this means for the life of the whole church and for congregational life. In the real world of real people and real faith communities, where does this lead? Even if the things you have read are persuasive, what is the effect in any congregation (for instance, your own) where not all members are in agreement?

The questions are appropriate. A great many pastors and church members are hesitant to take on the issues involved in the church's study and discussion related to sexuality, to "rock the boat" in congregations already afloat in local issues and parish programs. Many members may quietly wish for statements of welcome and actions that express acceptance, but are uncertain as to how and when to bring up an issue that may disclose a wide range of opinion and arouse some firm negative response. Some, of course, will gradually and quietly remove themselves from active membership. Many in the younger generation, doubtful about the relevance of the church, will see silence on the issue, or subtle messages of unwelcome directed toward LGBTQ friends and family members, as confirmation of their doubts.

In the conviction that welcome is central to our mission, let us turn to specific recommendations, and address them in some detail.

Recommendation 1: That in every effort to address the societal issues concerning sexuality, the church move the focus away from issues of sexual orientation and gender identity and focus instead on issues of behavior.

The focus on sexual orientation and gender identity in the political arena and in the church has tended to divert attention from a host of concerns more related to heterosexuality than to homosexuality: violence against women, teen pregnancy and sex education, women and children in poverty, sexually transmitted diseases, gender discrimination and sexual harassment, struggles of single parents, battles over abortion rights, promiscuity, pornography, sex in advertising, etc. All of these are *human sexuality* problems rather than *sexual orientation* problems, but to the degree that they can be attached to orientation, most of them are more to be identified with heterosexuality than homosexuality. So long as church and society focus on non-heterosexuality as "the problem," these other serious issues receive too little attention.

Recommendation 2: That every congregation take time for thoughtful discussion of Scripture and science as those relate to sexual orientation and gender identity, with a goal of coming to a clear declaration that there is welcome and a place at the table for LGBTQ persons.

Earlier in this book, mention was made of our *abridged* Bibles, our tendency to see and read and quote passages we have long known and regarded as foundational. But there is more to the Bible, and we will only enter this conversation fully if we involve ourselves in reading and discussing a wide range of texts, including some that are difficult and disquieting, and some that an earlier age may have read literally but that we no longer read in that way. I assure you, a generation that has read *Left Behind*, has been fascinated *by The DaVinci Code*, and has heard of the Jesus Seminar can handle it. Be willing to talk about what members of the group believe and think and wonder about the Bible, and talk about texts that show us the struggles of the writers; and then think together about how we see the inspiration of the Holy Spirit in the process.

It is easier to work with the Bible than with the sciences, simply because virtually every member will have a Bible. Fewer will have access to material from the sciences, and fewer still will have a basis on which to evaluate such material. If the congregation lacks a member who is able and adequate to lead the discussion, look to community resources. One area that awaits further examination is the relationship between suppression or denial of sexual orientation or gender identity and such personal or family issues as depression, family violence, various boundary violations, and even anti-social and criminal behavior.

From time to time we read or hear supposedly stunning stories concerning public figures – often public figures who have bannered their opposition to the "gay lifestyle" – who are caught in compromising situations: now a member of Congress, now a religious leader, now a Senator, next.... What the stories have in common is the degree of denial, shame, and self-hatred that accompany the "outing" of these individuals. From one perspective, they are receiving their just deserts. But I think of the stories more in terms of tragedy. In my view, if the persons involved were able to accept themselves as they are, and their sexual orientation as it is, they and the network surrounding them could be much healthier, more whole, and very likely less subject to inappropriate behaviors.

As this process is begun, one very significant question is what is to be gained or lost in discussion and decisions to welcome people of various sexual orientations and gender identities.

It is easy to identify what may be lost. First is the possibility that members with long-held convictions and prejudices against non-heterosexuals will leave the congregation. Second is the possibility that the discussion itself may create or expose divisions that will prove difficult to heal. Third is that neighbors or neighboring congregations may ridicule or caricature the congregation as being biblically unfaithful, as being "the fag church," or as being otherwise less "Christian" than alternative congregations. And, fourth, some members may fear the loss of the financial contributions of other members who do not agree with the congregation's stance or actions, a weighty list, to be sure.

So, what may be gained? First is the opportunity to truly encounter one another in deeper dialog than may have happened for many years, if ever. Second is the possibility that members will feel safe in discussing with one another the strains that have existed in their family circle, or the grief over one who has died of AIDS, or the love for a LGBTQ sibling or child, or questions and struggles best discussed with a Christian sister or brother. Third is the possibility that deeper exploration of the Bible will bring the Scriptures alive in a new way as we read and discuss. Fourth is the possible discovery that neighbors both gay and straight are looking for a church as inclusive in its ministry as Jesus was in his, a church in which a clear welcome expressed for LGBTQ persons can be read as a true declaration that the congregation is focused on ministry that goes beyond respectability and "birds of a feather" cohesiveness. Fifth is the significant but seldom-noted retention of members who would otherwise leave because of disillusionment with a church that is less gracious than they wish it to be. Sixth is the message given to youth and young adults that the church does not shrink from growth through encounter with them and the issues of their generation. Seventh is the possibility of actual growth in membership and contributions. And eighth is the possibility of prejudices overcome and hearts opened and warmed as members come to see former "strangers" as faithful and gifted sisters and brothers.

Recommendation 3: That denominations establish clear procedures by which non-heterosexual ordained or rostered persons, or candidates for ordination or rostering, may form faithful, committed relationships which can be recognized and accepted as such by the church in all its various expressions.

Consider the case of Ronald,[17] who hopes to be restored to the clergy roster. All who know him – including his congregation, his colleagues, his bishop, and the official group that voted to remove him from the roster – acknowledge his excellence in ministry, his personal integrity, and his faithfulness in relationship. But at present, his same-gender relationship trumps all other considerations, and he is considered unfit to serve. Or think of Arden, with a deep love for the Lord, for the church, for justice ministry. He worked for a church agency, but realized, with anguish, that the church would not accept him for ordained ministry because of his orientation, and his personal integrity would not permit him to conceal or be dishonest concerning this part of his life. His service to the Lord now takes place in a corporate setting, where there is (ironically) greater acceptance. And Marcia has pondered the possibility of seminary, but waits and wonders whether there will be a time that the church will receive her gifts for ministry.

The current policy of the ELCA, paralleled in other denominations, is what is known as a classic "Catch 22," a term that came into currency on the basis of a book (subsequently made into a movie) with that title[18]. The "Catch 22" of the story concerned the process for getting out of the military on the grounds of mental instability. The release could only be obtained by asking for it, but asking for a release established one's mental

---

17 With the exception of Andrea and Lauri, all names appearing in the recounting of pastoral anecdotes have been changed. All, however, are real people, and the situations described are real.

18 Heller, Joseph. <u>Catch 22</u>. New York: Simon & Schuster, 1961.

competence. One could not get a release without making the request, nor by making the request.

The church policy requires celibacy *apart from marriage* or faithfulness *in marriage* of all ordained or rostered personnel . . . but, of course, there is no liturgy or procedure by which the person who is not heterosexual may marry. Hence, there remains only required celibacy, a circumstance fervently condemned by the Reformers.

I am well aware that politicians and religious leaders opposed to acceptance of non-heterosexuals have done much to make the word "marriage" a touchstone of their orthodoxy. They have made "gay marriage" a term politicians might call a "third rail" (too risky to touch), named after the electric-current-conducting rail of an electric vehicle such as a subway car. Nevertheless, I continue to regard "marriage" as the most appropriate and recognizable term for persons joined in a recognized, committed, faithful relationship. I recognize that many who have been sensitized by way of the political posturing that has taken place, or who are still working through their views of sexual orientation, are unwilling to accept the term. The problem is that we have to call those relationships by some name! I await an alternative that is not "second class," but conveys full acceptance, equality, and respect. As stated earlier, my wife and I live in a marriage relationship that is not diminished by others who live in similar relationships under the same title, nor enhanced except in this way: our relationship is acknowledged and respected, and other people have some sense of who we are, what to call us, how to relate to us, on the basis of the familiar term. It is generally true that when we encounter "unmarried" couples – of whatever gender configuration – we are a bit uncertain as to how we should address them, how to treat them, in what ways to include them, even what "rooming arrangements" should be made when they are guests in our homes. And, perhaps, how to "gift" them on special occasions. Are they in some way two "singles," or are they truly a couple?

And, more than that, how are they treated in the church? Are they fully respected? Or is there a bit of hesitation as we try to make judgments regarding the "quality" of their bond and relationship? Will we list their anniversaries in the church newsletter, and honor the marking of 5 or 25 or 50 years together? A congregation dear to my heart lists the anniversary of a lesbian couple each year, and in all other ways recognizes their relationship as being as fully authentic as any that bear the traditional term, "marriage."

"Tradition" says that "marriage" means one man and one woman. But tradition is not always and automatically a positive thing. It would be easy to cite a list of times and societies in which "tradition" played a very negative role. As one long married, I am delighted to live under the umbrella of marriage (*"vive la difference"*). But things can change, new traditions can be born, new ways of thinking and new ways of using language can emerge. Each person must choose, of course, whether or not to feel diminished by equal rights granted to another. I would choose to see the use of "marriage" in this case as a joyous expansion of the circle.

Recommendation 4: That denominational policies and official statements be established or amended as required to permit the ordination or rostering of LGBTQ candidates on the same basis as heterosexual candidates, and with the same expectations for godly living and faithfulness in committed and recognized relationships.

This is really the crux of the matter. As noted earlier, the ELCA and some other denominations have extended a somewhat tentative welcome to non-heterosexuals to become members of the church and participants in the organizational life of congregations, but have been unable and unwilling to bring themselves to complete acceptance of these sisters and brothers as qualified to serve in rostered ministry. Many straight members who are comfortable at the level of "welcome" are less comfortable with seeing non-heterosexuals serving as ordained or rostered leaders. Within that discomfort lie the Bible verses we dealt with in an earlier chapter as well as assumptions about the supposed "lifestyle" of LGBTQ persons, and difficulty in surmounting the ingrained view that there is something innately "sinful" about being other than heterosexual. As mentioned once before, I would urge all involved in consideration and discussion of sexuality issues to give careful attention to the Commandment against bearing false witness (8th in the Lutheran numbering). Too many falsehoods and false assumptions are perpetuated by those among us who would continue to deny full equality to persons who are not heterosexual.

Clearly, this is a divide that will not be easily or quickly resolved. In the first decade of the 21st Century there are numbers of congregations being served by pastors and rostered leaders who are LGBTQ, and many more who would consider extending a call to qualified non-heterosexual candidates. But there are many – in fact, many more – that would not be willing to consider such a step *at this time*. For some, the time might never come. But let me emphasize, under ELCA polity (and that of some other denominations); that is, according to constitutions and established call procedures, *no congregation will ever be served by a pastor that is not called by vote of the congregation, or (in the case, for example, of interim ministry) that is not approved by the congregation's elected leadership.*

But let us take this one step further, and ask what may be gained or lost in a denominational decision to ordain or roster candidates who are LGBTQ. The first and most daunting potential loss is the loss of congregations, or even the fracturing of the denomination as congregations choose to avoid the struggle and take their stand on the long-held convictions and prejudices mentioned earlier. As this is written, in 2008, leaders of the worldwide Anglican Communion are striving mightily to avert division as congregations and dioceses withdraw on the basis of disagreements over issues of gender and homosexuality.

In other denominations as well, some who see non-heterosexuals as immoral and lacking appropriate boundaries have expressed their anxiety that the church's life and mission will be crippled by massive liability settlements in the future if the church moves toward full acceptance.

Division of the church, I am convinced, is an offense against the one God and Father of us all who has bound us together as a community with "one Lord, one faith, one baptism." We are members one of another, and every bishop, pastor, rostered leader, and church member is called to work for and manifest the unity in Christ given to the church "so that the world may believe."

But I wonder if it is not a worse offense for the church to sacrifice the reconciling and forgiving power of the gospel and retreat from that part of its mission which commits it to "strive for justice and peace in all the earth." It is a grave offense to draw back from seeking a place at the table for members hindered by long-held prejudice. The ELCA, in 2005, committed itself to live faithfully together in the midst of our disagreements. Some understand that action to mean acceptance of the status quo, no change in the policies or practices of the church. I and many others understand it as a call to open the door to a place at the table and in the rostered ministries of the church for LGBTQ members.

But what is to be gained from full acceptance of non-heterosexual clergy? I have already made clear my conviction that thoughtful and honest reading of the Bible does not preclude LGBTQ persons from full membership and involvement in the life of the church, including the pastoral/ministerial office. On that basis, I see as the first gain the full participation of people whom the Holy Spirit has "called ... through the gospel, enlightened with ... gifts, and sanctified and kept ... in the true faith." (wording from an earlier edition of Martin Luther's <u>Small Catechism</u>.) People who have felt the call to ordained or rostered ministry and have gifts to be shared in such ministry could be a tremendous resource if fully permitted to exercise their gifts.

In the second place, what is to be gained is honesty – integrity reclaimed! The church (and this applies to all denominations) has always had non-heterosexual clergy, but the price of ordination was silence, life "in the closet" with all the resulting stress and conflicts of conscience involved in such a life. Non-heterosexuals who felt called to ministry and who possessed Spirit-bestowed gifts for ministry could only exercise those gifts at the cost of some loss of integrity. And congregations were often complicit, concealing or denying their suspicions and perceptions in order to receive the ministry.

Further, because the entire structure of denominations required silence and a blind eye, congregations were prevented from full knowledge of the sexual orientation or gender identity of candidates. In my years of leading staff ministries, I was twice challenged as to the sexual orientation of unmarried pastoral associates, and treated the questions as inappropriate, though on only one of the occasions having clear knowledge on which to base my reply. If it was not a barrier to ordination, not only would the issue of sexual orientation soon lose its emotional dimension, but such information could be shared openly within the interview process. In the Lutheran church, each congregation calls its own pastor, following a process of review and interview. Openness would be widely welcomed, though acceptance across the church might be slow, as it was, for example, when the LCA and ALC began ordaining women. But it would happen, and pastors, congregations, and judicatories would all be the beneficiaries.

In the third place, what is to be gained is the trust of many people of all sexual orientations and gender identities who desire a community of faith more interested in "the ministry of reconciliation" (2 Corinthians 5:19), in "welcom(ing) one another as Christ has welcomed you" (Romans 15:7), than in focusing on the flaws of others in community or congregation. To be sure, some may be people motivated by the spirit of an age in which "everyone is OK and everyone's going to heaven," or in which each simply "does her or his own thing"; but others are people who have fully grasped the significance of Luther's teaching that the Bible is the cradle which holds the Christ, and their eyes are much more firmly focused on Jesus than on Leviticus.

I think that would be a very good thing!

In the Introduction, I referred to Marty Haugen's hymn, titled, "All Are Welcome." It opens with the words, "Let us build a house where love can dwell and all can safely live...." The words of the title are repeated three times in the refrain, "All are welcome, all are welcome, all are welcome in this place." If we hear those words as a declaration, a claim of singer or community that "that's the way it is," the words are and have been – for the great majority of Christian communities – manifestly untrue. But I would propose another way of hearing those words. Because God's grace is sufficient, and God's welcome inclusive, the church is called to make organizational decisions that permit it to more fully reflect God's grace and participate in God's welcome. And it is called to address individual and community attitudes that might hinder that grace and welcome.

I would propose that we hear the words of the hymn as the church's recognition that this is our calling. And we can sing our yearning for the Spirit's presence and power to be at work in us, keeping alive in us a vision of the church yet to be, where, indeed, "All *are* welcome in this place," and each has *A Place at the Table*.

(Turn to the next pages for a short list of resources.)

Resources

On the following pages are some resources I developed "along the way" while leading congregations through a process of education and discussion as part of the ELCA's study of sexuality and homosexuality. They include:

– a handout to help people identify their own preliminary view of and response to homosexuality

– a handout containing a *very* brief look at the "significant seven" passages most often quoted in opposition to homosexuality.

– a handout inviting people to begin wrestling with the question of how *consistent* they are in the way they read and understand the Bible.

– an outline of the steps to be taken and the hurdles to be surmounted for a candidate to be ordained in the ELCA.

– a brief explanation written in response to the request of a pastor who asked how to talk to young children about the commitment ceremony of a lesbian couple.

What is Homosexuality?

What is your understanding of homosexuality? To what may we liken it?

(Where would you place yourself on this line?)

1	2	3	4	5	6	7
Diversity		**"Flaw"**		**"Disorder"**		**Perversity**
"God made me this way"		"In a fallen world, this is the way I am"		"Bad people/ events have made me this way"		"I choose to scoff at God"
Analogy		**Analogy**		**Analogy**		**Analogy**
left-handedness		near- sightedness		rape or incest survivor		rapist

For Discussion

Many people see homosexuality as not in accord with the physical design (creation) of male and female sexuality in which genital design is complementary. If we accept this as a statement of fact, we would then ask:

Does this mean homosexuality is evil? Does it make one less a loved child of God?

Are committed homosexual relationships harmful to homosexuals? In what way?

In what way is homosexuality harmful to heterosexuals?

What harm would come to the church through full inclusion of non-heterosexuals?

What harm to society would result from legal recognition of homosexual relationships?

Further Statements for Reflection and Discussion

* no genetic basis has been found for either heterosexuality or homosexuality
* for millenia, homosexuals have been rejected and persecuted, and still today homosexuality is a criminal offense in scores of countries
* some homosexuals are extremely promiscuous
* some homosexual couples have lived together in love and faithfulness for decades
* some heterosexuals are extremely promiscuous
* some homosexuals are confused about their sexual identity
* some heterosexuals are confused about their sexual identity
* in the area of child-rearing, of all "parenting configurations", homosexual males are
  most likely to maintain a home with a stay-at-home parent
* on the face of it, homosexuality runs counter to the physical design of male and female
  sexuality
* some homosexuals have served as models of spirituality, faith, and religious
  commitment
* some heterosexuals see homosexuals as sexual predators and view them with alarm
* the majority of social scientists believe sexuality exists on a continuum, and that "no one is100% anything"

Biblical Texts Related to "Homosexuality"
The "Classic Seven"

Genesis 19:1-11 (4-8) "... the men of the city, the men of Sodom, both young and old, all the people to the last man, surrounded the house, and they called to Lot, 'Where are the men who came to you tonight? Bring them out to us, so that we may know them.' Lot went out of the door to the men, shut the door after him, and said, 'I beg you, my brothers, do not act so wickedly. Look, I have two daughters who have not known a man, let me bring them out to you, and do to them as you please; only do nothing to these men, for they have come under the shelter of my roof.'"

Judges 19:16-30 (22, 25) "... the men of the city, a perverse lot, surrounded the house, and started pounding on the door. They said to the old man, the master of the house, 'Bring out the man who came into your house, so that we may have intercourse with him.' ... So the man seized his concubine, and put her out to them. They wantonly raped her, and abused her all through the night until the morning."

Leviticus 18:22 "You shall not lie with a male as with a woman; it is an abomination."

Leviticus 20:13 "If a man lies with a male as with a woman, both of them have committed an abomination; they shall be put to death; their blood is upon them"

Romans 1:26-27 "For this reason God gave them up to degrading passions. Their women exchanged natural intercourse for unnatural, and in the same way also the men, giving up natural intercourse with women, were consumed with passion for one another. Men committed shameless acts with men and received in their own persons the due penalty for their errors."

I Corinthians 6:9-10 "Do you not know that wrongdoers will not inherit the kingdom of God? Do not be deceived! Fornicators, idolaters, adulterers, male prostitutes, sodomites, thieves, the greedy, drunkards, revilers, robbers – none of these will inherit the kingdom of God."

I Timothy 1:9-11 "… the law is laid down not for the innocent but for the lawless and disobedient, for the godless and sinful, for the unholy and profane, for those who kill their father or mother, for murderers, fornicators, sodomites, slave traders, liars, perjurers."

Alternate Views and Texts

In both Genesis & Judges the issues are violence, abuse, rape, and humiliation of the outsider – unrelated to the question of homosexuals in committed relationships. In Judges, the concubine is raped, abused, and ultimately killed – a victim of *heterosexual* violence.

Leviticus forbids conduct we would call "homosexual." Note that other words translated "abomination" are used in Leviticus and Deuteronomy for harnessing two kinds of animals together, planting two kinds of seed in a field, wearing clothing made of two kinds of fabric, and men wearing women's clothing or women, men's. Do we recognize the cultural element in these "laws"? Do we have a holistic view of the "purity laws?"

In the early chapters of Romans, Paul points out that "all have sinned and fall short of the glory of God", in order to underline the incredible good news that "they are now justified by his grace as a gift, through the redemption that is in Christ Jesus." Verses 26-27 are part of a long list including idolatry and "… evil, covetousness, malice … envy, murder, strife, deceit, craftiness, they are gossips, slanderers, God-haters, insolent, haughty, boastful…." In this long passage, St. Paul makes it clear that all are equally guilty, and when we condemn others, we also condemn ourselves.

"Vice lists" as in I Corinthians and I Timothy are intended to deter Christians from idolatry and licentious living. Yet we should note that our society seems to accept "the greedy" and have a new understanding of "drunkards." More to the point, there are a great many non-heterosexual Christians who are not "lawless and disobedient, ... godless and sinful, ... unholy and profane," and anyone who applied such terms to them might well be guilty of malice and slander, violating the 8ᵗʰ Commandment (refer again to the list in Romans 1).

SEE ALSO:

John 15:12 "This is my commandment, that you love one another as I have loved you."

Romans 13:9-10 "The commandments, 'You shall not commit adultery; You shall not murder; You shall not steal; You shall not covet'; and any other commandment, are summed up in this word, 'Love your neighbor as yourself.' Love does no wrong to a neighbor; therefore, love is the fulfilling of the law."

Galatians 5:14 "For the whole law is summed up in a single commandment, 'You shall love your neighbor as yourself.'"

Homosexuality and the Bible

We have identified four basic positions, or opinions, relative to homosexuality. We have termed them:

"Perversity"   a chosen evil
"Disorder"   the result of negative life experiences
"Flaw"   an unchosen, perhaps in some sense unfortunate, factor in one's identity
"Diversity"   one among many created alternatives

Because the church's life and teaching are based on the Bible, a very important consideration is:

How Do You Deal with the Bible?

Look at the following passages. In each case, do you *Agree* or *Disagree*? Explain.

- Women should be silent in the churches. (I Cor. 14:34)

- Any woman who prays or prophesies with her head unveiled disgraces her head (I Cor. 11:5)

- You shall not let your animals breed with a different kind; you shall not sow your field with two kinds of seed; nor shall you put on a garment made of two different materials. (Lev. 19:19)

- All who curse father or mother shall be put to death. (Lev. 20:9)

- For by grace you have been saved through faith, and this is not your own doing; it is the gift of God -- not the result of works so that no one may boast. (Ephesians 2:8-9)

- You shall not steal; and you shall not keep for yourself the wages of a laborer until morning (Lev. 19:13)

- Give to everyone who begs from you, and do not refuse anyone who wants to borrow from you. (Matthew 5:42)

- You shall not round off the hair on your temples or mar the edges of your beard.... You shall not ... tattoo any marks upon you. (Lev. 19:27-28)

- Whoever divorces his wife, except for unchastity, and marries another commits adultery. (Matthew 19:9)

- For the whole law is summed up in a single commandment, "You shall love your neighbor as yourself". (Galatians 5:14)

- The commandments, "You shall not commit adultery; You shall not murder; You shall not steal; You shall not covet"; and any other commandment, are summed up in this word, "Love your neighbor as yourself." Love does no wrong to a neighbor, therefore, love is the fulfilling of the law. (Romans 13:9-10)

- This is my commandment, that you love one another as I have loved you. (John 15:12)

- But as for the towns of these peoples that the LORD your God is giving you as an inheritance, you must not let anything that breathes remains alive. (Deut. 20:16)

- A woman shall not wear a man's apparel, nor shall a man put on a woman's garment; for whoever does such things is abhorrent to the LORD your God. (Deut. 22:5)

- You shall not plow with an ox and a donkey yoked together. You shall not wear clothes made of wool and linen woven together. (Deut. 22:10-11)

- If a man is caught lying with the wife of another man, both of them shall die, the man who lay with the woman as well as the woman. So you shall purge the evil from Israel. (Deut. 22:22)

- If a man meets a virgin who is not engaged, and seizes her and lies with her, and they are caught in the act, the man who lay with her shall give fifty shekels of silver to the young woman's father, and she shall become his wife. Because he violated her he shall not be permitted to divorce her as long as he lives. (Deut. 22:28-29)

- Those born of an illicit union shall not be admitted to the assembly of the LORD. Even to the tenth generation, none of their descendants shall be admitted to the assembly of the LORD. (Deut. 23:2)

- Suppose a man enters into marriage with a woman, but she does not please him because he finds something objectionable about her, and so he writes her a certificate of divorce, puts it in her hand, and sends her out of his house; she then leaves his house and goes off to become another man's wife. Then suppose the second man dislikes her, writes her a bill of divorce, puts it in her hand, and sends her out of his house (or the second man who married her dies); her first husband, who sent her away, is not permitted to take her again to be his wife after she has been defiled; for that would be abhorrent to the LORD, and you shall not bring guilt on the land that the LORD your God is giving you as a possession. (Deut. 24:1-4)

- If men get into a fight with one another, and the wife of one intervenes to rescue her husband from the grip of his opponent by reaching out and seizing his genitals, you shall cut off her hand; show no pity. (Deut. 25:11-12)

The Path to Ordination
Evangelical Lutheran Church in America

(Though not an official document, this list has been reviewed by recently ordained pastors)

Step 1 - Sense the call of the Holy Spirit to ordained ministry, read "What Shall I Say?", perhaps attend a "Called to Service" event as part of process of discernment.

Step 2 - Be registered by an ELCA congregation

Step 3 - Write an autobiographical essay on one's spiritual development

Step 4 - Undergo a psychological evaluation

Step 5 - Be accepted by the Candidacy Committee of that congregation's Synod

Step 6 - Be accepted for enrollment in a seminary program approved by the Candidacy Committee

Step 7 - Pursue a course of Theological Education under the review and supervision of the Candidacy Committee, with at least one year spent at seminary of the ELCA

Step 8 - As part of one's theological education, complete a program of Clinical Pastoral Education (CPE) to develop pastoral skills and do extensive self-analysis/ evaluation

Step 9 - Receive the endorsement of the Candidacy Committee to continue on the path toward ordained/rostered status

Step 10 - Complete a one-year internship, under an assigned supervisor, in an ELCA congregation or other approved ministry such as a chaplaincy

Step 11 - Receive approval for ordination from the Candidacy Committee and from the Seminary faculty

Step 12 - Be assigned to one of the ELCA's Regions and assigned to / accepted by a Synod

Step 13 - Receive a Letter of Call from a congregation of the ELCA after an interview process and a 2/3 vote of the members voting at a congregational meeting.

Step 14 - In the Rite of Ordination, pledge oneself to teach and preach in accord with the Scriptures, the Confessions, the constitutions of the ELCA and the congregation, and to "set the believers an example" in faith and conduct, understood to include conformity to the ELCA's statement of "Vision and Expectations".

"But What Do We Say to the Kids?"

A simple explanation of a same-sex commitment ceremony

Andrea & Lauri

Lauri and Andrea love each other and they share with each other their love of Jesus. They worship together, pray together, and study the Bible together.

It is true that most women fall in love with men and most men fall in love with women. But some people fall in love with people of the same sex – women with women, or men with men. That has happened to Lauri and Andrea. We don't know why that happens and they don't either. But they want to live with each other and always love each other.

They want the church, where people love and help and pray for each other, to love and help and pray for them. And we want them to know that we love them and like having them be part of our church, where we can pray with them and for them. They help all of us know that the church is a place where all people can feel welcome and can really believe that Jesus loves them.
We want everyone, all kinds of people, to:

> live among God's faithful people.
> hear the word of God and share in the Lord's Supper,
> proclaim the good new of God in Christ through word and deed,
> serve all people, following the example of Jesus, and
> strive for justice and peace in all the earth.

Andrea and Lauri can't get married, because you can only get married if you have a marriage license from the state, and right now the state only gives a marriage license if the couple consists of one man and one woman.

But Lauri and Andrea can make promises to each other that they will live together in love and faithfulness. And we can be happy for them, share their joy, celebrate their love, pray for them, and encourage them to keep their promises to each other and to God.

Bibliography

The bibliography could be expanded to immense proportions. I choose to offer a brief listing that I think would be of help and guidance to anyone wishing to read further.

Bloomquist, Karen, and John Stumme, eds. <u>The Promise of Lutheran Ethics</u>. Minneapolis: Fortress Press, 1998.

Brueggemann, Walter, William C. Placher, and Brian K. Blount. <u>Struggling with Scripture.</u> Louisville & London: Westminster John Knox Press, 2000.

Childs, James M., Jr., ed. <u>Faithful Conversations: Christian Perspectives on Homosexuality.</u> Minneapolis: Fortress Press, 2003.

Chilstrom, Herbert W., and Lowell O. Erdahl. <u>Sexual Fulfillment</u>. Minneapolis: Augsburg Fortress, 2001.

Evangelical Lutheran Church in America. <u>Journey Together Faithfully, Part Two</u>. Chicago: Evangelical Lutheran Church in America, 2003.

Hultgren, Arland, and Walter F. Taylor, Jr. Background Essay on Biblical Texts for "Journey Together Faithfully, Part Two: The Church and Homosexuality". Chicago: Evangelical Lutheran Church in America, 2003.

Jersild, Paul. Making Moral Decisions. Minneapolis: Fortress Press, 1990.

Maitland, Sara. A Joyful Theology. Minneapolis: Augsburg, 2002.

Menninger, Karl. Whatever Became of Sin. New York: Hawthorn Books, Inc. 1975.

Miller, Ed. Homosexuality and the Bible. (unpublished) Boulder: University of Colorado, 1999.

Seow, Choon-Leong, ed. Homosexuality and Christian Community. Louisville: Westminster John Knox Press, 1996.

Via, Dan O., & Robert A. J. Gagnon. Homosexuality and the Bible, Two Views. Minneapolis: Fortress Press, 2003.

Wink, Walter, ed. Homosexuality and Christian Faith. Minneapolis: Fortress Press, 1999.